Faith in Doubt

Faith in Doubt

Non-Realism and Christian Belief

David A. Hart

MOWBRAY

Mowbray
A Cassell imprint
Villiers House, 41/47 Strand, London, WC2N 5JE
387 Park Avenue South, New York, NY 10016–8810

First published 1993

British Library Cataloguing-in-Publication Data
A catalogue record for this book is available from the British Library.

Library of Congress Cataloging-in-Publication Data
Applied for.

ISBN 0–264–67327–1

Phototypeset by Intype, London
Printed in Great Britain by
Biddles Ltd, Guildford and King's Lynn

Contents

There lives more faith in honest doubt,
Believe me, than in half the creeds.

Alfred Lord Tennyson, *In Memoriam A.H.H.* (1850)

The Real is what will strike you as really absurd.

W. H. Auden, *For the Time Being* (1944)

Foreword

Citing Schleiermacher, Wesley, Bushnell, Barth and Martin Luther King, Jr as examples, the former head of Yale Divinity School in the United States, Dr Leander Keck, has suggested that the renewal of theology in the Christian church will come not from professional theologians but from preachers in the field. That is because it is the preacher who is driven to become a theologian in order to make sense out of his or her daily life and work. Professional theologians, Keck suggests, will not be the source of renewal since they have the luxury of debating ideas instead of being forced to live those ideas out in a very practical world. Hierarchical religious figures will also not be the source of the church's renewal, Keck asserts, because they cannot escape their distorting need to protect the institution that empowers them.

In many ways David A. Hart, in this book, illustrates this principle. As the Senior Anglican Chaplain at Loughborough University, David lives and works within the confines and world view of that science- and technology-oriented learning centre. I have been privileged to be his guest for visits on that campus. I have seen in him a man whose humanity attracts students and faculty, administrators and staff into his orbit of influence. They come out of every conceivable religious background and out of no obvious religious background. Yet time and again, in their relationships with David Hart they receive that greatest of gifts, the validation of their humanity and the enhancement of their being. Those gifts are not just the accidental contributions of a great and sensitive man who happens to be an Anglican priest. They are rather the results that emerge when David Hart lives out his theological commitments in his workplace and through his relationships.

In preparation for his life's work he has grounded his very being in the classical disciplines of his profession. He has been shaped by the likes of John Macquarrie and Dennis Nineham of the Church of England, as well as by Cornel West and Tom Altizer from the American theological scene. But what these scholars gave him was not a fixed body of 'revealed truth' but rather a point of view out of which he would grow, and the rare theological courage to journey beyond the fearful boundaries that many believers erect at the edges of their systems of faith. Like many other disturbers of institutional religious peace, including especially his mentor and friend, Don Cupitt of Emmanuel College, Cambridge, David Hart has walked beyond these faith edges into the churning sea of doubt, uncertainty and insecurity. He has faced honestly the limitations of human language that tend to mark the faith commitments of twentieth-century men and women. Yet he walks with the integrity of being both an honest believer and a critical, even doubting, thinker. Above all, he walks as a dedicated Christian. In the words of the Psalmist this man is seeking a way 'to sing the Lord's song in a strange land'.

In this magnificent small book, David Hart shares his inward journey in a public way. Under the guise of examining various theological claims of yesterday, he looks at the authority patterns of the religious past that guarded the standard claims of orthodoxy and created security while impeding both human growth and human maturity. He seeks the meaning behind the religious words that flow far too easily from the lips of those with an unexamined faith tradition. He calls his readers into the exhilarating freedom that dares to ask the questions and to roam into issues and places where most religious thinkers refuse to go. The context of his life as a chaplain, dealing with real people and real concerns, is never lost. His is the theology of a preacher who must communicate with ordinary people who raise ordinary questions as they try to make sense out of their lives each day. It is therefore, an incredibly readable book.

There are few David Harts in organized religion in the world today. When we discover one of them in our midst we must encourage and support him or her, even while we celebrate the life of so special a person. For such people are pearls of great price upon which the Christian church must depend if it hopes to live with power and integrity in the twenty-first century.

The Rt Rev. John S. Spong
Bishop of Newark, USA

Acknowledgements

Acknowledgement is due to the copyright holders for permission to quote the following extracts: the lines from T. S. Eliot's 'Choruses from *The Rock*', W. H. Auden's 'September 1, 1939' and 'Leap Before You Look', and the extracts from David Hare's *Racing Demon* and W. H. Auden's *Secondary Worlds* are reproduced by permission of Faber & Faber Limited; extracts from Deryck Cooke's *Gustav Mahler: An Introduction to his Music* are reproduced by permission of Faber Music; extracts from the *Journals and Papers* of Søren Kierkegaard, edited by Howard V. Hong and Edna H. Hong, are reproduced by permission of Indiana University Press; extracts from Søren Kierkegaard's *Concluding Unscientific Postscript*, translated by David F. Swenson and Walter Lowrie, Søren Kierkegaard's *Either/Or*, translated by David F. Swenson, Lillian Marvin Swenson and Walter Lowrie, and Richard Rorty, *Philosophy and the Mirror of Nature* are reproduced by permission of Princeton University Press; the line from David Bowie's 'Changes' is reproduced by permission of RCA Limited, Record Division. The preface to Holy Communion by Ronald Pearse is reproduced by his kind permission. I would like to thank Stephen Mitchell for allowing me to quote his comments during the BBC *Heart of the Matter* debate in the press. Thanks also to the Ven. Dr Harold Lockley, first chaplain of Loughborough College, for his help with the Bonhoeffer material.

Introduction

For twenty years I have wrestled with questions of faith and doubt and have tried to discern the connections between them. There was a time when I believed they were in direct opposition. Those of us who come from traditionalist church backgrounds have been reared on that understanding. And under that fallacy (as I now see it) the traditionalist answer is always: to affirm the faith and repress the doubt. But the difficulty with that course of action is the inevitability of what Freud called 'the return of the repressed'. The doubts do not disappear. So, rather than push them down as soon as they emerge, I now believe that the better course is that we should let them arise, feel their shape, look them squarely in the eye, take them on board, so that we can learn to live honestly with them. This, in my experience, is more likely to produce a spiritual equilibrium than the repressive prescription we were previously given. As Robert Browning expressed it through the character of Bishop Blougram:

> With me, faith means perpetual unbelief
> Kept quiet like the snake 'neath Michael's foot
> Who stands calm just because he feels it writhe.[1]

The ritual of regular churchgoing tempts us to a false sense of security. It tempts us to believe that God and the belief-structure are unchangeables and our task is to fit in with those. We are the only changeable element. I grew up in the 1960s in a traditional Anglican parish where the Book of Common Prayer of 1662 was as important a fixed and authoritative script as the text of the Bible. In such a setting I fell in love with the majestic world of church language and rituals. But I knew all the time that there were parts of myself that had no place in that very closed world, and that that world did not want me to express. I had a sympathy for rebellious and extreme people, partly of course because inside myself I came to discover a rebel and an extremist. I have admitted to be being a child of the 1960s and so many of us felt as I did.

I was fortunate that in the 1970s I came under the influence of questioning and caring institutions and individuals who helped me to clarify my world intellectually. Dennis Nineham was the Warden of my Oxford college, Keble, and Professor John Macquarrie supervised my theological research and inspired me with his combination of Anglo-Catholic spirituality and existentialist theology. He was also instrumental in allowing me to spend a year at Union Theological Seminary in New York, where Professors Cornel West and Tom Altizer awakened my eyes and ears to postmodern questions.

In the 1980s I lived and taught in a number of remarkably different locations in Britain, and I soon discovered that the questions that continued to plague me were commonly felt by others too wherever one moved, and in being ordained I discovered they were asked as much 'inside' Holy Orders as 'outside'. Don Cupitt provided almost a book a year in this decade, helping many of us to focus our thinking in a network called Sea of Faith which was built up around his writings and ideas.[2]

In the 1990s I have become Anglican Chaplain of Loughborough University, and have been privileged to host the monthly meetings of the East Midlands Sea of Faith group in our university chapel. Although this is largely an older group, I soon discovered that many of our students are engaged in a similar wrestling match, between their inherited beliefs and their radical questioning. I am deeply indebted especially to the members of the Loughborough Students' Anglican Society and the weekly Human Enquiry Group of Hazlerigg-Rutland Hall who allowed me the privilege of sharing doubts and faith both theirs and mine.

Twenty years ago David Bowie wrote a song called 'Changes' which sums up well for me (as no doubt for others) the intervening years. It includes the line 'Time may change me, but I can't trace time'.[3] I would like to thank Bishop John Hughes, formerly Bishop of Croydon, who confirmed and ordained me, for tracing my time of changes through so patiently with me over the past twenty-five years. Although I know already he will not agree with my arguments for a non-realist perspective on faith, he will read my case carefully and take it to heart.

Judith Longman of Cassell encouraged me warmly from the start of this project and I would like to thank her for her enthusiasm. My colleague the Reverend Sue Field encouraged me to keep in touch with my feelings as well as my intellect. That is important. Seth Kasten, Head of Reader Services at Union Theological Seminary, helped me patiently to find references, and Lois and Porter Kirkwood goaded me on from Oyster Bay. From Germany, Birgit Lautenschläger-Knorzer reminded me of the limitations of God the Father. My friend Simon Storey helped me research and patiently word-processed the manuscript. Barry Sweetman of Wolfson College, Cambridge prepared the indexes.

To my parents I owe most, for they disagreed about God but stayed together.

David A. Hart
New York City
Feast of the Transfiguration 1992

Notes

1 *The Poetical Works of Robert Browning* (John Murray, 1929), vol. 1, p. 537.

2 Membership of which has doubled this year (1992) following a BBC programme on Easter Day featuring three 'doubting' clergy from Loughborough.

3 Initial track from David Bowie, *Hunky Dory* (RCA Record Division, 1971).

1 What is 'non-realist' faith?

It is when I said,
'There is no such thing as the truth',
That the grapes seemed fatter.[1]

Faith in our century in the West has come of age. By this, I mean that it has, after a period of considerable questioning and self-criticism, come to a stage where it can, independently of its traditions, stand up and show itself to be that developed, sophisticated but flawed, human creation that it is. Although it has always been claimed to come from above, and consequently to possess divine origin, in the maturity of its current perceived form we can see and examine the all too human origins and genetics of our faith.

> The great god Pan is dead. (Pascal)

One of the essential components of this new understanding of faith must include the earlier theological insight that a traditional external deity outside our universe can be of no further use to us at this stage of our religious development. We may be able to transcend the anxious news of God's demise but we cannot deny the decisive significance of his eclipse not only in our contemporary society at large but also in the world of our own spirituality if we see ourselves as men and women of faith. In Martin Buber's image, God has 'gone to the catacombs'[2] and he will not be returning from them again.

If we wish to have a responsible spirituality ourselves and to be in a position to offer such to our contemporaries, we have to take the implications of this on board in every respect. It is a philosophical position which will have significance in our doctrine, in our politics and ethics, in our worship, and in our hopes for the future. We have to learn to leave go of theological images which in their naïvity are damaging to the greater maturity we have achieved through the efforts of biblical scholars, psychologists and social critics of religious systems. To an earlier generation this century the great New Testament commentator Rudolf Bultmann suggested that one could not switch on the wireless and in the next moment of consciousness revert to a belief in exorcism (presupposing that demons lurked behind bushes). This would be to live on an unstable and even schizophrenic mental plane. How much more valid becomes the force of his argument in the age of the microchip, when computerization gives us instant access to the history of faith heretofore, as every other branch of knowledge, and jet travel enables us to enculturate ourselves in religious world-traditions of our choice virtually anywhere on the globe.

Those of us who grew up in the West in the time after the World Wars have come at considerable cost to realize the danger of any one ideological position attempting to command universal respect. Such attempts to produce a monolithic explanation have been doomed to an inevitable failure, as the actual world of our lived societies is a plural world of many different beliefs and social patterns and in such a world as this there has to be allowance made for such diversity. No one group has the right to believe itself absolutely correct in its beliefs or to be the only community in existence with a God-given identity.

If we accept this then we have to accept also the inevitable cultural relativity of all our philosophical, religious and political viewpoints. Linguistic philosophy has surely convinced us this century of the power of words to structure our realities, and although those words are developed within our groupings, we have no access to any meaning of those words which lie 'outside' their respective groups. Because all our language is developed in our cultural groups, the only articulation we can make of what we perceive to be true is through the medium of language. Being a human medium, it is flawed and gives us no immediate access to any world beyond or outside that of our own verbal structuring.

For this reason, our faith can no longer be shored up by an understanding that we have an absolute revelation uniquely granted. As Bishop John Spong has expressed it, 'Every identification of the truth of God with any human group's understanding of the truth of God will finally have to be surrendered'.[3]

Following on from this point, no one religious or life perspective can any more claim the unique privilege of a relationship with the deity giving it a special circumvention of the natural workings of the universe as we have discerned it in contemporary science and history. Earlier forms of such a claim gave a reassuring consolation to the believers who saw themselves in a protected world, privileged by their share in the saving faith. Such an attitude has of course been shown by countless religious groupings, many with incompatible beliefs, but the claim of a privileged protection as a perk of membership of the group has had a similar emotional appeal to all who have subscribed to whichever creed was on offer at the time. The Psalmist expressed the arrogant joy of such knowledge of belonging: 'A thousand shall fall at thy side, and ten thousand at thy right hand; but it shall not come near thee.'[4]

A maturer understanding of faith denies the believer such easy immunity from suffering. Indeed at the heart of Christianity, in the image of the cross, is perceived a contrary indicator, of the inevitability of suffering and its central location in the drama of salvation. Only by embracing such suffering in the fullness of its humanity can we discover any quality of a redemptive life in the image set before us.

In the course of this book we start from the position known as 'non-realism' which owes a lot to structuralist philosophy.

Its implications for Christian belief have been explored and developed in the corpus of works by Don Cupitt beginning from his book in 1980, *Taking Leave of God.*[5] Without attempting to argue the full case here for that position, the following perspective is one that the author shares with a considerable number nowadays, both inside and outside the church and loosely connected ideologically by a number of groups devoted to Cupitt's writings and their implications. Meeting in centres throughout Britain, and loosely known as the Sea of Faith Network, we share a common concern to understand religion, Christian as much as any other, as a human creation, not, of course, owing our existence to any single authors but dependent on the creative spiritual interpretations of the universe and the self as historically articulated by individuals and groups. We have a regular newsletter and an annual conference. Beyond that, there is no single agreed code of theory or practice. Diversity is celebrated by those who subscribe to such a creative view of the capacity of the human spirit, the capacity we each have within us to define and refine what creates us and binds us together spiritually.

Such a position as ours has an inevitable ambivalence. There is a human nostalgia for a past time which evinced a greater certainty that God was in his heaven, and all was well on earth. St Paul regarded the Torah as the schoolmaster who brought Jews to Christ that they might be justified by faith.[6] So now we regard our Christian inheritance as a further stage in the development of our faith, as human co-creators taking responsibility for our beliefs as much as for our actions. Like Prospero in Shakespeare's *The Tempest*, our experience has projected us to a necessary final sacrifice. We remain fully cognizant of the power and significance of the magic we have now abjured for the sake of a new and fuller humanity we believe we have discovered through a greater and more detailed study of our experience. It is a mature judgement that Prospero makes at the end of the play and one that presupposes a richness and diversity of experience, as observed not only by the characters in this drama but assumed in the life of the Bard himself:

> Now my charms are all o'erthrown,
> And what strength I have's mine own.[7]

Faith yet reveals under our new understanding a more positive and helpful visage. True to the earlier dynamic understanding of faith as revealed in the biblical story of Abraham setting out towards the unknown from the familiar Ur of the Chaldees, we now embark on a similar pilgrimage of our own in which, in the words of the author of the letter to the Hebrews, 'Faith is the substance of things hoped for, the evidence of things not seen'.[8] We know what we have glimpsed of what was called 'the divine', but our starting point now is that the location of this vision was our own human potential *tout court*. Nothing was given from outside, since all human believing is a product of our common human consciousness.

Such a position is often taken by orthodox believers as being rather negative, even destructive, in its denial of divine existence. But on the contrary, it can be both argued and experienced as a positive renewal of confidence in the human spirit, which we each share in, and its creative potential for good. Such a difference of interpretation is well revealed in characteristic good humour by Woody Allen in his film *Stardust Memories* in which a critic chides a producer with the charge 'We don't want an Easter film by an atheist'. And comes the speedy reply: 'To you I'm an atheist; to God I'm the loyal opposition.' Although the argument is that it is no longer helpful to conceive of God as a supernatural existing Being 'out there', it is from a central loyalty to our Judaeo-Christian tradition that we would wish to maintain much of the language and many of the insights of that tradition, albeit transposed into an entirely different key, from the supernatural to the natural entire.

Such a key change frees us from the subordinate conscious-

ness which has so dominated thinking in our religion as elsewhere in the history of our consciousness, and which has been
most fully evinced and criticized in G. W. F. Hegel's works of
the nineteenth century.[9]

In the following attempt to expound a non-realist understanding of faith, the author's particular perspective as a writer from
a particular part of the West and a particular time of the second
half of our century cannot be gainsaid. It is in fact one of the
major presuppositions of the position here promoted that there
is no such thing as a non-perspectival or absolute religious
position. Accepting this does not, however, in any way imply
that there cannot be a wider agreement among those of differing
perspectives, who nevertheless share a common situation of
contemporary time and culture. There is an association of ideas
and values that can have a cogency which compels, by what
the philosopher Ludwig Wittgenstein called the 'family resem-
blance'. For this reason, a commonly agreed radical programme
is necessary if we wish to free misconceptions about faith from
the constrictions of past time and practices.

One example only need suffice here. If we believe that all
our religious constructs are in fact human creations, then it is
incumbent upon us, whatever our exact viewpoint as individuals, to listen sympathetically to the modern feminist cri-
tiques of religion, in their argument that all religious traditions
up to our own day are demonstrably the products of male and
patriarchal perspectives. If men have constructed societies and
their religions until now, then a non-realist perspective will
want to challenge that bias and to offer a sympathetic ear to
those men and women who today offer us alternative gender
models to perceive the divine and to consider the effect these
have on our human perceptions of sexuality.[10] But the stories
are as important to listen to as the ideologies, and so it is time
for the current author to reveal how he came to hold his own
non-realist position.

A discovery of the essential truth of a non-realist theological

position can be a pleasant or an uncomfortable personal discovery, just like the discovery of any other human truth. For
myself, I recall vividly the moment when this truth became the
truth *for me*, and it was a moment of pure joy.

But first, a working definition of 'non-realism' as provided
by the Sea of Faith Steering Committee:

> The view that there is nothing beyond or outside human
> beings, neither God nor some other notion like 'Ultimate
> Reality', that gives life meaning and purpose. We do that
> for ourselves.[11]

I was twenty-two and was walking on a beautiful summer's
day to a temporary job I had at a watermill in the tiny hamlet
of Bagnor in Berkshire, a watermill converted into a small
theatre which housed a hundred people at a maximum. I was
on my way to an evening's work in the theatre restaurant. As
I walked through the green lanes of that verdant county, I
recited to myself the joyful words of the audacious prophet
Zarathustra, 'He who with eagle claws grasps the abyss, he has
courage'.[12]

I realized at that moment the joyful truth that, as my life lay
before me, there was no other person than myself who would
take responsibility for the shaping thereof. There were parents,
there were teachers, there were friends and colleagues, but the
connections I had with them were subject to *my* will, and I was
not subject to the will of any other authority, in particular, one
that had foreknowledge of my every action and influenced my
every movement and that, as an idea, had been very influential
in my teenage years, namely the concept of a sovereign personal
God, the Creator of all (and me in particular) who also watched
over one's every action and would finally judge everyone for
what they had done in this life. At that moment I realized the
full emotional implication of what I had already taken on board
intellectually, namely that that concept was only a product of

7

my inflated super-ego and therefore had no further power over me or control over the destiny that lay before me. 'God is Dead' was the Nietzschean formula and in assimilating the significance of that death for myself on the Bagnor road, I simultaneously discovered my life, or a new dimension of that life, which I had not known before, and best characterized by the term 'freedom'.[13]

Escape from authority is always a liberating experience, especially so when the authority has been viewed as absolute in its extent and its exercise.

The Christian religion, in common with its monotheistic relations Judaism and Islam, has in its traditional forms exercised such a mode of authority as would perpetually remind its adherents of their status as created 'subjects' who owe their very being to the divine will. In Judaism, the most significant part of the lawcode begins 'I am the Lord your God, who brought you out of the land of Egypt, out of the house of bondage. You shall have no other gods before me.'[14]

Is this not a case of escape from one form of servitude straight into another type of slavery? Whereas in Islam (whose very name means 'submission') there is a daily routine of ritual prostrations which clearly indicate a hierarchical type of belief, in the Christian religion the focus of authority varies with the brand. The authority can be vested in the words of the biblical narrative or the magisterial authority of the church. It matters not. The significant point is the very postulation of an absolute authority over and against the individuals who are called to submit completely to its power.

This device exlains the otherwise inexplicable alliance that has grown up in recent years between traditionalist catholics and conservative evangelicals. They are prepared to sink their (fairly considerable) doctrinal differences in order to oppose the common enemy. Neither dares to countenance a form of belief which would want them to take responsibility for the creation of their own beliefs. Both wish to subject their respective adherents totally to a commonly agreed authority, not so much because that authority leads one to the truth, as that submission to authority is *per se* the path to salvation. If some truth is not yet known, it is perhaps not meant to be known. The authority, be it book or person, has deemed it inappropriate for the truth to be perceived by this particular people and/or in this particular time. In this way of thinking there is usually much talk of revealed truths. But the other side of this coin (although one never acknowledged as such) must be that in this authority are concealed or revealed truths that are 'not fit for human consumption'. Such a disdain for the human intellect is all par to the course, and one of the reasons why many regard the dissolution of all religious authority as the inevitable outcome of human and rational enlightenment. So in his work *Against Religion*, the until-recently Christian A. N. Wilson rejects the imposition of any absolute authority in religious systems which bring to the fore a figure such as the Grand Inquisitor, be that figure represented by Billy Graham or a John Paul II.[15] The power exercised by such a figure has, Wilson argues, a dual quality, 'the power to console, and the power to inflate indignation'.[16] In a world come of age, to use the expression forged by Dietrich Bonhoeffer, it would not any longer be legitimate for religious institutions to wield these types of power, for the consolation would be inadequate and the inflammation of indignation unnecessary.

The power of religions to manipulate moral outrage in societies has been enabled by their use of the twin social tools of shame and guilt. Criticisms in the traditions of Marx and Freud have allowed us to see how subjective these devices are, particularly as they seem to have been developed as an emotional underlining of prevailing cultic and sacrificial systems that would keep individuals and societies subservient to the claims made by these respective religious traditions. Like all means of control, they have been considerably effective tools in keeping believers in line, but it is difficult for us now to see how guilt, often based on irrational forces within, can be positively used by an enlightened religious attitude to life. In the majority of cases individuals seem left with groundless and negative feelings about their own self-worth which simply reinforce a low self-esteem, and such feelings of inadequacy are scarcely helpful for any teaching about faith which claims to be life-giving. How, we will ask in this book, can faith be exercised with a due regard for the worth of the self as well as allowing the exercise of appropriate religious authority?

A contemporary understanding of authority which is to take such criticisms into account must take cognizance of the Enlightenment critique of Immanuel Kant (1724–1804), who rejected heteronomous ethics, which found their authorization in an object beyond self, in favour of autonomous ethics which took proper account of the value and claims of the individual human self. Kant postulated the existence of a 'transcendental something = X' and therefore left open the possibility of the development of a theonomous ethical system.[17] In the words of Paul Tillich (1886–1965), 'Kant wanted to maintain the unconditional character of the moral demand against all emotional relativism, against fear and pleasure motives, as well as against divine and human authorities'.[18]

By establishing humankind under its own (autonomous) laws, Kant effectively 'rationalized' the ethical system of his day, and provided the means by which it was impossible, given his system, to bypass the laws of reason in the exercise of moral judgement. And this is precisely what traditionalist Christianity wishes to maintain.

A second thinker who has wrestled with these problems is Søren Kierkegaard (1813–55). Kierkegaard, true to the tradition of Martin Luther that he inherited, did not see faith as the appropriation of a solid body of doctrinal information but rather as 'an existential communication' which involved the participation of the believing self as much as the object in which the faith was entrusted, or to which it was directed. Kierkegaard's model of faith in fact replaces a static objective reality to which one can grant or withhold one's assent with a relational model which envisages a commitment made by the individual in a situation of uncertainty and considerable ambiguity.

Hence Kierkegaard's definition of faith is one which underscores the immense significance of the individual existing believer:

> Faith is the objective uncertainty due to the repulsion of the absurd held fast by the passion of inwardness, which in this [i.e. Christian] instance is intensified to the utmost degree. This formula fits only the believer, no one else, not a lover, not an enthusiast, not a thinker, but simply and solely the believer who is related to the absolute paradox.[19]

The authority of the Christian faith requires an object. For example, it requires the necessary historical information 'that in such and such a year God appeared among us in the humble form of a servant, that he lived and taught in our community, and finally died'.[20] This information is 'more than enough' for the purposes of the appropriating individual believer.

And the most effective way to communicate the truths of the Christian faith, in Kierkegaard's eyes, is not by the bold and blatant issue of external truths as orders, for this would not produce the sufficient and necessary engagement required by the individual believer. Kierkegaard anticipated much of the non-directive counselling philosophy of our own century when he wrote in his *Journal*:

> Authority does not mean to be a king or to be an emperor or general, to have the power of arms, to be a bishop, or to be a policeman, but it means by a firm and conscious resolution to be willing to sacrifice everything, one's very life, for his cause; it means to articulate a cause in such a

way that a person is at one with himself, needing nothing
and fearing nothing.[21]

Not only is Kierkegaard critical of traditional notions of
Christian authority, he even challenges traditional assumptions
about authorship in his project of the 'pseudonymous writings'.
Rather than conveying his often tentative theories about the
self and Christian faith under his own authorship (thereby
presumably giving them the authorization of his own signature),
Kierkegaard adopts a variety of pseudonyms for a number of
his works which have the effect of distancing the author from
his text, thereby emphasizing the greater responsibility of his
individual reader in relation to the theories being expounded.

Thus the meditation on the awesome story of Abraham being
prepared to sacrifice his only son Isaac, entitled *Fear and Trembling*, is written by John the Silent; Victor the Hermit provides
the title and preface of a work he has 'discovered' in a secret
drawer of some secondhand furniture he has bought, *Either/Or*;
Constantin Constantius provides the cool-headed psychological
analysis of *Repetition*; the retelling of Kierkegaard's own unhappy
love affair with Regine Olsen in *Stages on Life's Way: Studies by
Sundry Persons* is collected, forwarded to the press and published
by Hilarius Bookbinder. Most tellingly of all, when approaching
the detailed teachings of the Christian faith, two contradictory
pen-names are adopted which bring into question the whole
attitude of the writer towards the material upon which he is
engaged. Johannes Climacus was the mediaeval monk who is
alleged to have written *The Ladder to Heaven*. It is not clear how
far Johannes himself had ascended the ladder, if at all, and this
is therefore a fitting pseudonym for *Philosophical Fragments* and
Concluding Unscientific Postscript; while the contrary Anti-Climacus
takes responsibility for *The Sickness unto Death* and *Practical Introduction to Christianity*. Of *For Self-Examination*, one half was given
posthumous publication.

If a truth is to have authority then, to a certain extent, it matters not who initiates the idea, as long as it elucidates an appropriate response. Kierkegaard avoided the path of ordination in his own career because he believed that the institutional church often claimed for itself the authority of Christ that it had in fact abrogated by its actions. In the same way, in his writings he signed his devotional works personally, but in the corpus of his writings that attempt to unravel the issues of faith and life, he can only be true to his subject by adopting a number of different and sometimes conflicting personae.

In a sense Kierkegaard here puts his finger on the pulse of the twentieth-century postmodernist consciousness with its sense of the loss of the continuity of the self in the myriad of inhabited worlds. In a world that is much faster moving than the nineteenth-century Denmark Kierkegaard knew, we dwellers in the 1990s can perhaps feel a sympathy for the biographical confession of Victor the Hermit:

> When I consider the different periods into which [my] life falls, it seems like the word *Schnur* in the [German] dictionary, which means in the first place a string, in the second, a daughter-in-law. The only thing lacking is that the word *Schnur* should mean in the third place a camel, in the fourth, a dust brush.[22]

This modern perception concerning the radical discontinuity of the self brings into question the authority of dogmas if they are applied in a similar fashion as mathematical formulae. Because Christian teaching concerns faith and its development in the life of the individual believer, a complex web of intricate signals or a series of interlocking mirrors are more capable of expounding what it is that faith may adhere to. What is doomed to failure is the authoritative stance of the preacher or conventional sermonizer. In his work 'justifying' the pseudonymous authorship, Kierkegaard himself argues:

No, an illusion can never be destroyed directly, and only by indirect means can it be radically removed. If it is an illusion, that all are Christians—and if there is anything to be done about it, it must be done indirectly, not by one who vociferously proclaims himself an extraordinary Christian, but by one who, better instructed, is ready to declare that he is not a Christian.[23]

We have now reached the region of radical denial, of challenging the meaning of the word 'Christian', and of heavy irony, a world very familiar to many of us today. And, in this world, we must remember that 'When Christ drove the money changers out of the temple, he fashioned a whip of a rope. This whip he wielded with authority. The whip of satire is always without authority.'[24] Is it not the world of satire in which we feel most comfortably placed today?

The question I shall attempt to answer in this book is: what does it mean to hold a non-realist faith, to believe that language about God is really about the self, and that religious belief is part of the creativity we all share in as part of our humanity?[25] Clearly some translation is necessary, some transposition perhaps from the divine to the human key. But this is not surprising, is it? After all, is not this process at the very core of the whole enterprise of Christian theology, the attempt to translate the unspeakable things of God into the words of contemporary men and women? So, as T. S. Eliot put it, 'Christianity is always adapting itself into something which can be believed'.[26]

If Eliot is right, then Christianity is not, as traditionalists often model it, a castle of impenetrable and immovable beliefs built at some primaeval time by our forebears and only to be entered on the terms of their world-view. Such a static model of the relationship between divine and human truth is not even realistic in its portrayal of *how* the castle came to be built in the first place. Be it referring more to Bible or to church, the image fails to take account of the creative dynamic between divine revelation and human inspiration which shored the building up at the onset.

In addition, critics regard as 'the intentionalist fallacy' the commonly perceived idea that the true meaning of a text must have been in the mind of the writer as he or she perceived it, and that it is the sole job of successive readers and interpreters to rediscover and reclaim that original intention from the writer's mind. Even if such an exercise were possible, which it clearly is not (because of cultural divide), it would not be beneficial in the light of the insight derived from Kierkegaard that the individual subject is intricately involved in the creation and appropriation of existentialist meaning.[27] Simone Weil (1909–43) has brought out the point that the true meaning of any statement or story is quite other than the meaning the original writer intended. So she does not see an understanding of Christ as limited to the pages of Holy Scripture alone, and she can write of a passage from Sophocles which she has been translating 'The interpretation which sees Electra as the human soul and Orestes as Christ is almost as certain for me as if I had written these verses myself'.[28]

We may press Simone Weil to ask why she needed to have included the 'almost'. Is not the Christ perpetually discovered by generations of new Christians in the crucible of their own experience? At the beginning of our century after hundreds of pages attempting to pin down the christological figure in his *The Quest of the Historical Jesus*, Albert Schweitzer (1875–1965) came to this enlightened conclusion:

> He comes to us as One unknown, without a name, as of
> old, by the lakeside, He came to those men who knew
> Him not. He speaks to us the same word: 'follow thou Me'
> and sets us to the tasks which He has to fulfil for our
> time. He commands. And to those who obey Him, whether
> they be wise or simple, He will reveal Himself in the toils,
> the conflicts, the sufferings which they shall pass through

in His fellowship, and, as an ineffable mystery, they shall learn in their own experience Who He is.[29]

For Schweitzer this discovery led him away from the attempt to find Jesus Christ in books, out to the poor and ill on the African continent. He became a pattern in this way for many twentieth-century men and women of faith, who regarded the attempt by the church to enclose the figure of Jesus Christ within the pages of history or the closed doors of the ecclesiastical castle as futile and one that hindered their search for the truth.

The pages of biography and fiction alike in our century in the West are scattered liberally with the stories of priests and religious who have wrestled with the problem of where to find Jesus Christ and have decided that he has departed the places where he was traditionally and conventionally to be found. The tension between the traditionalist expectation of the priestly role and the true life of the Spirit is well conveyed in the scene at the opening of the film adaptation of Tennessee Williams's play *The Night of the Iguana*, when the young girl who has an attachment to Reverend Shannon says to him 'I'm sick of dark old churches. I like sunshine. Sorry, I keep forgetting what you were, what you are.'[30]

The commonly accepted image of Christ at the end of the last century, as one of oppressive and dominating doom and gloom, prompted the poet Algernon Charles Swinburne (1837–1909) to pen the lines:

> Thou hast conquered, O pale Galilean; the world has
> grown grey from Thy breath.[31]

Substantially as a result of this negative perception, the great critics of the Christian faith in the nineteenth century, such as Blake, Hegel, Marx, Dostoevsky and Nietzsche, pleaded for a more wholesome understanding of humanity than anything which could be derived from such a negative image as this portrayal of Christ. But, paradoxically, these critics were also inspired by much in the biblical and Christian tradition, and have therefore not only been among the most radical creators of modern atheism, but also proved to be seminally influential upon much twentieth-century Christian thinking.[32]

So in the true style of the Hegelian dialectic, the enemy has been brought within the castle and the occupants, in their quest for liberation, have embraced him and are willing to follow him in the path to a truer and a fuller understanding of the Christ within. Nowhere has this theme been better explored than in the film *The Poseidon Adventure* in which the traditionalist and the modern clergymen battle for the souls of those whose lives are threatened with imminent drowning, and those who are prepared to leave the security of the area they know (the dance floor) and follow the call of the modern pastor to the unknown territory of the (upturned) engine-room above are those who will at least have a chance to live. Those who listen to the counter-advice of the traditionalist priest to stay just where they were are soon wiped out completely. Although it seemed crazy to follow the advice to leave the place of comparative safety, it was in fact the only way to go.

Although many twentieth-century Christians have, in the insecurity of contemporary times, decided to embrace the structures of belief of a former age, and we have witnessed a considerable growth in the West in conservative evangelical churches and house-groups, the only way to a mature and integrated faith in these or any times is to accept the substantial thrust of the scientific and empirical knowledge of our particular age as the starting point, which would lay down the permissible boundaries of what may or may not be believed. Increasingly, Christian faith of the traditionalist type appears to be of the order of believing a thousand impossible things before breakfast: that the world was created in seven days; that the Bible is the literal and infallible word of God himself; that Jesus was born of a pure virgin; that he came down from the cross in bodily form; that ordinary diseases can be removed entirely by the laying-on of hands; that folk in world-faith traditions other than Christianity have no knowledge of the truth and are condemned to eternal punishment because they have not; that bisexuality and homosexuality is a curse, and AIDS part of God's righteous punishment on sinners; that at some future time angelic trumpets will play and the dead rise again. Such doctrines, commonly believed and taught by apparently sane people, nevertheless remain teachings totally at variance with the general scientific and empirical conclusions of late twentieth-century Western humankind. No one believes that any of these are possibilities in our ordinary world. So the only way in which they can be seriously held is to bring in the concept of 'miracle' and to suggest that these teachings arise from an entirely different world-view from our own. But is it ever a path of integrity to abandon the insights of one's own culture and generation at a particular point in favour of insights of another generation for a particular aspect of one's life and belief? This is exactly the sort of device that those, say, opposed to the ordination of women must be using when they admit that women have equal rights in our society, but then go on to declare that this does not apply in the sphere of the church since Jesus' choice of twelve male disciples is determinative of ecclesiastical leadership for all times and places. Such a form of intellectual schizophrenia is not only unnecessary but was also never previously required for those who were going to take up the Christian faith.

Why have such radical and dishonest devices become necessary in our day? Only, surely, because the gap between belief and unbelief has seen to become so wide, because traditionalist believers want only to shout louder their beliefs and to reinforce crudely the adage of Dean Inge that 'he who marries the spirit of his own age becomes a widower in the next'. But, on the other hand, who wants to marry a lifeless corpse? Who wants to embrace a set of unbelievable premises that they would never for one moment consider basing their day-to-day practical lives upon? The answer is, surely, only the timorous.

Better by far, and truer to our Judaeo-Christian traditions, to adopt the faith similar to Abraham: 'By faith Abraham obeyed when he was called to go out to a place which he was to receive as an inheritance; and he went out, not knowing where he was to go.'[33] It is in this spirit, I believe, that Don Cupitt quotes the words of Meister Eckhart in the work that began his series of radical reinterpretation of the Christian faith that inspired the establishment of the Sea of Faith Network: 'Man's last and highest parting occurs when, for God's sake, he takes leave of God.'[34]

And it is in this same spirit, of free and open engagement in the questions of our pluralistic modern society, that our present Archbishop of Canterbury spoke when he said that the church should become like a cathedral he had visited in Papua New Guinea, which had a roof, but no walls:

> I believe with all my heart that the Church of Jesus Christ should be a church of blurred edges . . . a church of no walls where people can ask their hardest questions without condemnation and share their deepest fear without reproach.[35]

Hard questions and deep fears abound in contemporary society and so surely it is in engagement with those that a true understanding of God must be found. From a non-realist viewpoint, God can no longer be regarded as an external personality that impinges on mine. 'Rather, God is the religious requirement personified, and his attributes are a kind of projection of its main features as we experience them.'[36]

On the basis that God does not exist as a person, he cannot take offence simply because we do not use his name. The name that we use for the religious requirement is less important than the experience encapsulated for the believer by the language. For this reason, the words in Tillich's famous sermon on 'The Depth of Existence' remind us that the importance lies in the conserving of the sense of the mystery, or the numinous, rather than in the recitation of any particular name:

> The name of this infinite and inexhaustible depth and ground of all being is GOD. That depth is what the word GOD means. And if that word has not much meaning for you, translate it, and speak of the depths of your life, of the source of your being, of your ultimate concern, of what you take seriously without any reservation. Perhaps, in order to do so, you must forget everything traditional that you have learned about God, perhaps even that word itself. For if you know that God means depth, you know much more about Him. You cannot then call yourself an atheist or an unbeliever. For you cannot think or say: Life has no depth. Life itself is shallow. Being itself is surface only. If you could say this in complete seriousness, you would be an atheist; but otherwise you are not. He who knows about depth knows about God.[37]

Although atheists can have this experience as much as theists, religious non-realists believe that the traditional language of God is the most helpful matrix for human beings to relate and connect with the deepest parts of themselves, and that this language is often useful in discovering the workings of the parts of ourselves that seem outside the scope of our rational control.

In a way it has always been accepted that language about God is a particular kind of language, *sui generis*, having a different status to that of ordinary human language. Traditional theology, following Augustine, described it as 'analogical', and in our own time, Ludwig Wittgenstein (1889–1951) wrote 'When we say "God sees us", we do not then go on to describe his eyebrows'.

With all languages, one is talking about one thing and using another word, a 'signifier', to use the contemporary jargon. The relationship between 'signifier' and 'signified' is forever dynamic, and we live in a time which has seen 'the disappearance of the transcendental signified'.[38] Rather than ignoring this, pretending that it has not happened, Christians should accept it as a fact of our common spiritual history, the point beyond which we have now reached on our pilgrimage, and by facing the full implications of the death of God (as a transcendent Other) we can rise to its challenge and incorporate it as a meaningful event in our history. At this point, some theologians have diverted the focus of our attention, either to the survival of religion in the secular city or to the importance of liberationist and prophetic strands in the Bible or to the rediscovery of the feminine in the Judaeo-Christian tradition.[39] Important though these issues are to the future of theology, they cannot detract us from the central metaphysical question of the existence of God. A theologian such as Tom Altizer has indeed been more consistent in using the insights offered by Hegelianism and postmodernism to reinterpret for human use traditional language about God. He sees no radical discontinuity between contemporary atheism and incarnational Christianity. They both proclaim the death of God and, for Altizer, 'to speak of God is finally to speak of speech itself . . . the voice of "I AM" is heard in the voice of "I Am" '.[40] The movement of the incarnation is a continued shift from the sphere of the divine to the human matrix. Rather as in the world of art through the Renaissance, an increasing stress can be traced on the detail of the human figure rather than the divine image.[41] The holy is found in the midst of human life rather than somewhere beyond it.

In this book I shall attempt an exercise in translation. I shall take a range of Christian doctrines and practices and attempt to show what they can mean for those who now believe that in speaking about God and the world beyond we are in fact speaking about ourselves, and discovering the roots of our personality and interpersonal communication. The central idea has been encapsulated in the words of the Australian novelist Patrick White: 'There is another world, but it is in this one.'[42]

It is also a smaller world of interpretation we inhabit today than we have dwelt in up to now, and any interpretation of God that is appropriate to the global village we inhabit has to be larger than that of the tribal deity which has until now been a feature of our religious horizon.[43] Whatever our tradition, we should make an effort to step out from it and embrace a vision that is coherent and takes into account the extreme diversity and great complexity of the human character.

The reputation of liberal theology is that it has in the past tended to produce an optimistic sheen over the human condition, often giving the impression of a blandness and a lack of engagement with genuine human conflicts. This is undoubtedly part of the inheritance of the Neoplatonic tradition, in which evil is interpreted not so much as a thing in itself as an absence of the good. Perhaps this goes to explain why dominant periods of liberalism can be abruptly ended by outbreaks of global darkness. For example, liberalism as a dominant ideology fell swiftly out of favour with the outbreak of the First World War, and again at the onset of the oil crisis in 1973.[44] Both ideologies were swiftly replaced by others of a more conservative mode, because liberalism was perceived to lack the resources to address the darker forces that were then seen to be amassing on the international horizon. This ideological deficiency had been grasped earlier this century by Thomas Mann in his novel *Doctor Faustus*:

> In my view 'liberal theology' is a *contradictio in adjecto*, a contradiction in terms. A proponent of culture, ready to adapt itself to the ideals of bourgeois society, as it is, it degrades the religious to a function of the human; the ecstatic and paradoxical elements so essential to the

religious genius it waters down to an ethical progressiveness. But the religious cannot be satisfied in the merely ethical, and so it comes about that scientific thought and theological thought proper part company again. The scientific superiority of liberal theology, it is now said, is weak, for its moralism and humanism lack insight into the demonic character of human existence, cultured indeed it is, but shallow; of the true understanding of human nature and the tragic nature of life the conservative tradition has at bottom preserved far more; for that very reason it has a profounder, more significant relation to culture than has progressive bourgeois ideology.[45]

A non-realist theology must not be a shallow ideology. It must take as true an account of 'the dark side of God' (as Jung put it) as of his goodness. This necessity was grasped by that great advocate of radical theology Bishop John A. T. Robinson in a personal way when in 1983 he was diagnosed in Cambridge with a terminal disease and said in his last sermon that 'we must learn to see God in the cancer as much as in the sunset'.

In what follows, I shall attempt to show how a non-realist theology can take fully into account the spectrum of human activities and provide an analysis of the range of what it means to be human. In doing so, we must be mindful of the insights provided by some of the earliest of the church Fathers, who sensed the oneness of God with humankind. St Gregory of Nazianzus, in stressing the centrality of the human nature of Jesus Christ, used the argument that 'that which he has not assumed, he has not healed'. Athanasius stressed the goal of the incarnation to be that 'God became man in order that man might become God'. Justin Martyr in his *First Apology* implied that the Logos could be present to some extent in all human beings. The full humanity of Jesus became, of course, a touchstone for orthodox definitions of the person of Jesus as they became schematized in the fourth century. Anything less than this was seen as a denial of the central truth of Christianity in the doctrine of the Incarnation.

By the process of 'interiorizing' Christian doctrines we can get a handle on the whole range of human experience and intercourse: being born and realizing dependence in the family unit; being educated and realizing the significance of knowledge; relating to others and fulfilling one's personal and sexual potential; coping with disease and deciding how to care for the weak; purchasing and consuming as partakers in the market; living with death and helping each other with our grieving. Such is the raw material of each of our lives and such is also the subject matter of our theological thinking and discourse. If Evagrius of Pontus (346–399) was right when he defined the theologian as 'the man [*sic*] who prays', then we must also remind ourselves that theology must not become overly cerebral. Sam Keen's book *To a Dancing God* reminds us that God is to be celebrated as much as (s)he is to be understood.[46] Theology and liturgy must always be mutual handmaids if they are to evoke the quality of our joyful existence in the created world.

And here we must return to another ancient insight, that theology is not primarily of service to the church (however that is defined) but is rather to be seen as a preparation for the Kingdom of God on earth. If the Kingdom (or 'the Commonwealth') is the primary category of gospel understanding (and it is certainly primary in the earliest gospel tradition), then it is by defining the work of each and all for the Kingdom that theology must finally be assessed, rather than providing ecclesiastics with comfortable rules of 'the club' by which they can reassure themselves and excommunicate others.

I have the sense that in some countries this task is being more effectively performed than in others. In the United Kingdom and in France, theology seems to have retreated into the service of the church and scarcely seems to venture outside the ecclesial world. In Germany and the United States, however, theology seems to be read in the wider world more, as literature and sociology are read. It is no coincidence therefore that *The Open Church* should be produced by a German theologian, and by a writer who has achieved international acclaim for integrating the concerns of church and world.[47]

By opening the church fully to the concerns of the world, theology will be better placed in this country to answer the questions that people are asking, rather than answering the questions that spokespeople for the church *think* that people should be asking.

In what follows, the attempt is made to apply the theological wisdom of the tradition to the concerns of our age. And underlining these concerns must be a common and honest appropriation of the truth of contemporary pragmatic atheism. For, whatever they might say in opinion polls, pragmatic atheism is the path that the majority today follow in our country, and this is a new situation for theology to address. As T. S. Eliot again succinctly expressed it at the beginning of the century:

> But it seems that something has happened that has never
> happened before;
> though we know not just when, or why, or how, or where.
> Men have left GOD not for other gods, they say, but for no
> god; and this has never happened before.[48]

Notes

1 Wallace Stevens, 'On the Road Home' in *The Collected Poems of Wallace Stevens* (Alfred A. Knopf, 1978), p. 203.

2 Quoted in Iris Murdoch, *Metaphysics as a Guide to Morals* (Chatto & Windus, 1992), p. 80.

3 Bishop J. S. Spong, *The Future of Christianity in the West* (Loughborough University, 1992), p. 11.

4 Psalm 91.7. All biblical references are taken from the Revised Standard Version unless otherwise stated.

5 Don Cupitt, *Taking Leave of God* (SCM, 1980).

6 Galatians 3.25.

7 Cf. the epilogue of *The Tempest*.

8 Hebrews 11.1.

9 Cf. especially G. W. F. Hegel, *Phenomenology of Spirit*, trans. J. N. Findlay (Oxford University Press, 1979).

10 Cf. the discussion of this matter proposed by Network groups as the major item of consideration for the Sixth Annual Conference at Leicester in July 1993.

11 From *Notes for Newcomers* for Sea of Faith III Conference (1990).

12 Friedrich W. Nietzsche, *Thus Spake Zarathustra* (T. N. Foulis, 1909), p. 353.

13 Cf. the perceptions concerning this in the challenging work by Hugh Dawes, *Freeing the Faith* (SPCK, 1991).

14 Exodus 20.2f.

15 In Dostoevsky's novel *The Brothers Karamazov*.

16 A. N. Wilson, *Against Religion: Why We Should Try to Live Without It* (Chatto & Windus, 1991), pp. 27f.

17 Immanuel Kant, *Groundwork of the Metaphysic of Morals* (Harper Torchbooks, 1976).

18 Paul Tillich, *Morality and Beyond* (Fontana, 1963), p. 72; in his *Systematic Theology* (James Nisbet, 1968), *passim*, he develops the idea of a theonomous ethic.

19 Søren Kierkegaard, *Concluding Unscientific Postscript* (Princeton University Press, 1941), p. 540.

20 Søren Kierkegaard, *Philosophical Fragments* (Princeton University Press, 1936), p. 87.

21 Søren Kierkegaard, *Journals*, ed. Howard and Edna Hong (Indiana University Press, 1967), vol. 1, p. 73, para. 183.

22 Søren Kierkegaard, *Either/Or* (Princeton University Press, 1971), vol. 1, p. 35.

23 Søren Kierkegaard, *The Point of View of My Work As an Author* (Harper & Row, 1962), p. 24.

24 Kierkegaard, *Journals*, vol. 1, p. 77, para. 189.

25 Don Cupitt describes such interpretation as 'symbolic and action-guiding': *Radicals and the Future of the Church* (SCM, 1989), p. 168.

26 Quoted in the Preface to John Hick (ed.), *The Myth of God Incarnate* (SCM, 1977).

27 As explored theologically in the works of Dennis Nineham, especially *Explorations in Theology* (SCM, 1977), vol. 1.

28 Simone Weil, *Attente de Dieu* (La Colombe, 1950), pp. 177–89; cf. *Letter to a Priest*, trans. A. F. Wills (G.P. Putnam's Sons, 1954), pp. 43–5, as quoted in Helen Gardner, *The Limits of Literary Criticism* (Oxford University Press, 1956), pp. 15f.

29 Albert Schweitzer, *The Quest of the Historical Jesus* (Macmillan, 1950), p. 403.

30 Tennessee Williams, *The Night of the Iguana* (Secker & Warburg, 1961).

31 Algernon Charles Swinburne, 'Hymn to Proserpine' in *The Poems of Swinburne* (Chatto & Windus, 1904), vol. 1, p. 69.

32 I owe this insight (among many others) to the American Tom Altizer, Professor of Comparative Studies at the University of New York, Stony Brook, here from his *The Gospel of Christian Atheism* (Westminster Press, 1966), p. 21.

33 Hebrews 11.8.

34 Meister Eckhart, sermon quoted on flyleaf of Cupitt, *Taking Leave of God*.

35 Quoted in *The Independent* (14 July 1992).

36 Cupitt, *Taking Leave of God*, p. 85.

37 Paul Tillich, *The Shaking of the Foundations* (Pelican, 1962), p. 64.

38 Mark C. Taylor, *Erring: A Postmodern A/Theology* (University of Chicago Press, 1984), pp. 103f.

39 Cf. Harvey Cox, *The Survival of Religion in The Secular City* (Macmillan, 1990); Gustavo Gutiérrez, *A Theology of Liberation* (Orbis Books, 1973), and many other writers, especially from South America; Mary Daly, *Beyond God the Father: Towards a Philosophy of Women's Liberation* (Boston Press, 1973); and in Britain, Daphne Hampson, *Theology and Feminism* (Blackwell, 1990).

40 Thomas Altizer, *The Self-Embodiment of God* (Harper & Row, 1977), p. 93.

41 Cf. especially here George Pattison, *Art, Modernity and Faith* (Macmillan, 1991).

42 Cf. the epigraph of Patrick White, *The Solid Mandala* (Penguin, 1974), as quoted by Bishop John A. T. Robinson, *The Roots of a Radical* (SCM, 1980), p. 9.

43 Cf. especially here the third part of the lecture delivered by Bishop Spong, *The Future of Christianity in the West*, pp. 14–17.

44 Cf. the preface to Karl Barth, *Epistle to the Romans* (Oxford University Press, 1933).

45 Thomas Mann, *Doctor Faustus* (Secker & Warburg, 1949), p. 90.

46 Sam Keen, *To A Dancing God* (Harper & Row, 1970).

47 Jürgen Moltmann, *The Open Church: Invitation to a Messianic Lifestyle* (SCM, 1978).

48 T. S. Eliot, 'Choruses from *The Rock*' in *Collected Poems 1909–1962* (Faber & Faber, 1963), pp. 177f.

2 *The resurrection and the dead*

> The right synthesis of death and life is what Christians call eternal life. The only religious meaning of death is death of the self.[1]

Easter Day 1992 made Loughborough well known for something other than its bell foundry and its sport. Following a BBC programme in which three local clergy talked about their disbelief in the physical resurrection, Loughborough became what was subsequently described as 'an epicentre of theological controversy'.[2] The programme was the regular religious feature *Heart of the Matter*, presented by Joan Bakewell. Two Anglican clergymen, Stephen Mitchell and David Paterson, and Catherine Middleton of the United Reformed Church, spent some time explaining why they did not believe that Jesus Christ rose from the dead, and even more time suggesting when and how they would share these doubts with their congregations.

Subsequent events were not easy for any of the three. The Anglicans were called to see their bishop in the midst of popular calls for their resignation, and although Catherine had been in Loughborough only for about a year, she moved on to another position after receiving a considerable amount of flak from her congregation. In the event, the two Anglicans were required to produce an apology for the upset they caused 'the faithful' and a retraction of much of what they had said on the programme, and the bishop in question called all his clergy together to lay down the 'minimal requirements' of belief.

All this controversy seems quite incredible in the light of the biblical criticism of the last 150 years. One of the first biblical critics, the German David Friedrich Strauss (1808–74), wrote that the best criticism of dogma is the history of dogma itself. His own work began the process of regarding all the supernatural elements in the gospels as 'mythical' rather than historical and this he applied most certainly to the stories of the resurrection of Jesus. Strauss came to believe all talk of life after death was in the realm of fantasy, and he gave strict orders that his own funeral rites be without ceremony; no bells, no books.[3]

The bishops who condemned the clergy who appeared in the programme probably had on their own shelves the sceptical conclusions of the leading scholars of the twentieth century. The leading New Testament scholar Rudolf Bultmann (1884–1976) wrote:

> If the event of Easter Day is in any sense an historical
> event additional to the event of the cross, it is nothing
> else than the rise of faith in the risen Lord since it was this
> faith which led to the apostolic preaching.[4]

And in the leading work of Anglican dogmatics, *Principles of Christian Theology*, Professor John Macquarrie stated:

> It is obvious that the resurrection is not an historical event
> in the same way that the cross is, that is to say, not a
> publicly observable event. It is meant to affirm that God
> acted in Jesus, and the earliest mentions of the
> resurrection speak of it as God's act, not Christ's. We have
> already seen plainly enough that an act of God is not a
> publicly observable event or a phenomenon open to sense
> perception, though it manifests itself in and through such
> occasions. Stories of the empty tomb and of accompanying
> marvels look like examples of the usual mythologizing
> tendency, which seeks to express the faith that God has
> acted in terms of objectifiable and empirically verifiable
> phenomena. Even if such stories could be proved to be

veridical accounts of observed events, they would not in
the least establish that God had acted in these events, for
no such evidence is relevant to such a question.[5]

Even without the benefit of modern biblical scholarship the
gospel stories of the resurrection appear anything but clear-cut
accounts of the rising of a physical body, and are at the very least
mutually incompatible accounts. With the insights of such higher
criticism, we are left seeing the stories as highly charged theologically, needing to be purged of first-century presumptions.

If we look within the authorized statements of Anglican doctrine, their story is more blurred than those who expressed
horror at the suggestion that the empty tomb might be a myth
would admit. Seventy years before the controversial *Heart of
the Matter* programme was broadcast, the official report of the
Commission on Christian Doctrine appointed by the Archbishops of Canterbury and York raised the historical question
as to whether antecedent beliefs developed within late Judaism
about the resurrection of the just on the last day might not
have influenced the shaping of the tradition within the New
Testament of the resurrection of Jesus:

> This consideration inclines some of us to the belief that the
> connexion made in the New Testament between the
> emptiness of a tomb and the appearances of the Risen Lord
> belongs rather to the sphere of religious symbolism than
> to that of historical fact.[6]

If such a suggestion was acceptable in 1922, one might well
ask why its articulation in 1992 should cause such conster-
nation. This point seems to have been glimpsed by Archbishop
George Carey when he weighed in on the debate and alluded
to the difficulty of tying down the biblical accounts into one
type of explanation. During the course of the debate he said
in a sermon in Chesterfield parish church 'The mode of the

resurrection is tantalizingly unclear: Christ's body appears to have properties which transcended the earthly body of Jesus; he appears and he disappears'. Of course he still went on to insist that the doctrine was rooted in 'historic Christianity' but that is what archbishops are expected to say at such a juncture in a public doctrinal debate.[7]

And here we have to face the fact that the physical raising of the dead so they walk around again is simply not part of the credible inhabited Western world of our time. Our scientific and medically knowledgeable culture rejects as invalid the attempts of earlier cultures to divide humankind into dualistic characteristics (body and mind, soul and spirit) and thereby to allow the possibility that one element could have a life independent of the other. We no longer deem it credible that the mind could leave the body and at some later stage be reunified with it. The self is one. And when the body dies the soul/spirit dies with it never to be reunited for some new task. So the twentieth century takes to itself the words of the Greek poet Pindar: 'O my soul, do not aspire to immortal life, but exhaust the limits of the possible!'[8]

If we want to have an indication of this, we need to look no further than the Funeral Service as authorized by the Church of England. In the rite revised for inclusion in the Alternative Service Book (1980), the focus has shifted significantly from the earlier Book of Common Prayer (1662) to rest almost entirely not on the deceased but on the gathered mourners. So the opening prayer seems to slide over the coffin from the objective reason for the gathering to the alleged faith of those gathered around it:

> Heavenly Father, in your Son Jesus Christ you have given us a *true* and a *sure* hope. Strengthen this faith and hope in us all our days, that *we may live as those who believe* in the communion of saints, the forgiveness of sins, and the resurrection to eternal life.

In qualifying 'faith' and 'hope' in this way, and in the three-fold reiteration of alleged beliefs, it appears that the congregation are being given reassurance and the focus is put on their belief rather than any held by the deceased. It does not seem to matter, throughout the remainder of the service, what beliefs, if any, the deceased held. Perhaps the revisers were canny enough to reckon that it was statistically unlikely that the majority of those departing via the rites and practices of the Established Church would hold any such religious beliefs anyhow. But certainly at the end of the service we come back to the main object of the pastoral care being exercised. The final prayer of the minister before the Committal reads: 'Grant *us*, Lord, the wisdom and the grace to use aright *the time that is left to us here on earth*', and even the blessing is taken from the form 'Unto him that is able to keep *us* from falling. . .'.[9]

When I used to take duty crematoria funerals on a regular basis, I used to flinch from saying some of these prayers. What a presumption it was on my part as the minister, I thought, to assume that these folk whom I had never met before had these types of beliefs, and that in their grieving for their loved one now laid before us for the last time, I should voice what purported to be their beliefs and what they hoped to achieve or fulfil in the remainder of their own lives. It was not really up to me to speak of such intimate things on their behalf. Small wonder it was therefore that there scarcely ever seemed to be an audible 'Amen' when it was requested of the congregation in the Alternative Service Book text.

As a university chaplain, I do not often perform funerals. I am sometimes asked to take memorial services, usually to bring parents and other family over to the campus setting to share with them and the student friends of the deceased some of the happy memories of the individual's life and contributions of the university community, and something of the pain of having to say goodbye and let go together. Often there is the planting of a plaque or a tree as a memorial and a visible symbol for the deceased's memory. I feel much more comfortable taking these memorials.

Gone in them is the frenetic repetition of reassurances about the afterlife and the massive concern to remind everyone of their faith and their hope. Perhaps the greater distance in time, or the space away from the place of burial, has liberated the situation. But the focus lies much more naturally on the beloved and their life; their friends and their music are there as part of the liturgy, which has often been created by friends, and their participation is offered as a quiet but effective witness of loyalty and love. The minister's role here is a much more comfortable one, as MC and co-ordinator of the general grief rather than as divine spokesperson and justifier of the (clearly here per-ceived as cruel) ways of God to men. Partially, I think, the difference is that, with a student generation in a multi-faith society, no one would presume as to their intimate beliefs in quite the way that the authors of the ASB Funeral Service deemed it appropriate. The unspoken assumption would be that in the case of university students only a few of them would be self-proclaimed Christians, and even of those a number would not hold with any belief in an 'afterlife'. And so the equation becomes a less rigorous formula, a more relaxed recipe. And, as on all such occasions, what is spoken from the heart creates more resonance than what is repeated (by rote) from the head or the book.

Because our contemporary beliefs are best represented by art, I would like to take four examples from this area—from the plastic arts, from literature, poetry and from music—to illustrate what people believe in our times about resurrection. The artist Stanley Spencer (1891–1959) lived and worked in the peaceful Berkshire village of Cookham. His paintings have a deep religious quality, many of them being scenes from the life of Christ acted out with the faces and in the dress of the contem-porary villagers of Cookham. Many local people recognized themselves in his paintings, perhaps with a measure of surprise as they saw themselves portrayed as fishermen or as attendant disciples listening to the Sermon on the Mount. But in Spencer's view it was as essential to Christianity as to art that the ordinary was the place where the extraordinary appeared. Christ was modelled on an ordinary villager; he was originally a carpenter from a small community, and in that state of humility it was believed the divine dwelt. There is no other place that God can dwell but this world, there are no other people he can use but everyday folk; in Spencer's work, it is a case of 'heaven in ordinarie' as the poet George Herbert (1593–1633) expressed it.[10]

Spencer concentrated a number of his paintings on the theme of the general resurrection. *The Resurrection in Cookham* (hanging in the Tate Gallery) is the first in this theme which Spencer later continued to develop in his *Port Glasgow Resurrection* series. In his first painting, the setting is clearly the graveyard in Cookham parish church. The wall of the church is visible as a backcloth and in the main part of the picture we see the graves of the deceased—singles, couples and families, who are helping one another rise—most of them in their Sunday best but one or two of them buried more clearly in paupers' uniform or even naked, as the circumstances of their individual demise must have dictated. Our gaze takes us straight away to the appearance and demeanour of the ordinary folk of Cookham parish who now are being granted a miraculous 'second bite' at their lives, and are getting up as if after a long and satisfying sleep. Although the idea is thereby miraculous, the world is not miraculous at all. Or rather, it is neither more nor less miraculous than the world of rural Berkshire, or later of industrial Port Glasgow, that we already know and love. And so the world in which the resurrection happens looks like the ordinary world we know, *this* world, and the people who inhabit it are the ordinary, mostly not so very good-looking or angelic, people that we meet and know. Spencer's point is explicitly that the resurrection is a this-world and present-life experience and there

is little 'romantic' feel about another world or even a transformation into anything of a different order. It is in the humdrum
world that we are raised up, or rather (particularly in the rather
more crowded Glaswegian location) help one another rise up.
Is there not something in the biblical tradition to the effect that
the disconsolate and the downcast among the disciples had their
spirits relieved and raised by those who told them with joy their
recent experience of 'seeing the Lord'? And so the spread of the
good news of the resurrection was also in its very essence the
passing on of the word of extreme encouragement of those who
felt depressed and abandoned. A pervasive sense of social joy
is reflected from the canvas of Spencer's works. And it is a joy
that he connects specifically with his Christian vision, though
a vision firmly rooted in the Kingdom of heaven on earth.

> In this life we experience a kind of resurrection when we
> arrive at the state of awareness, a state of being in love,
> and at such times we like to do again what we have done
> many times in the past, because we do it anew in
> Heaven.[11]

Our next example of the experience of resurrection is the
novel of that name by the great Russian writer Leo Tolstoy
(1828–1910). The story told concerns the wealthy Prince Nekhlyudov who in the course of an adventurous youth meets a
peasant girl of fifteen and leaves her with a 100-rouble note
and a child. Their second meeting is traumatic indeed for the
Prince who is now exercising his authority in the region as a
judge. By coincidence, the woman appears before his bench as
a prostitute, which force of circumstances has made her become.
As she appears, Tolstoy gives full vent to his powers of dramatic
description and picks out the detail of the woman's skin as
'of that whiteness peculiar to people who have lived long in
confinement'.[12]

The novel then concentrates on the worry and guilt that

Prince Nekhlyudov feels for his previous victim as he is now called upon, ironically, to judge her. But out of the whirlpool of emotions he feels comes a gradual experience of rebirth as an individual moral being, of resurrection. In a sense Nekhlyudov becomes a new man through what he suffers in his emotional turmoil because in that moment of the second meeting with the woman she appears to him in a new light. The change that occurs in him is an open change, not one that can be easily characterized or described. So, we are told, 'How this new period of his life will end, time alone will prove'.[13]

Being open to the unknown but exciting future is clearly also present in the layers of the biblical story of the raising of Jesus from the dead. The eleven frightened men who locked themselves behind closed doors 'for fear of the Jews', through the story they received and believed about the resurrection of Jesus, became fearless missionary pioneers who left the security of their own counsel and Jerusalem to take a radical message of hope to the far ends of the known world of their time.[14]

Tolstoy's novel on resurrection is inspired by the gospel story but not confined to it, to one particular understanding of how life is renewed. He speaks from and towards a culture which is his own, and from a story with which his readers can identify he distils an essence of universal religious truth about the nature of human life which is ever renewing itself and rising up, phoenix-like, from the slough of a previous despair. The other element which is clearly critical to the understanding of this particular story is that the rebirth is not brought about by any conscious efforts on the part of Prince Nekhyludov. Indeed it is the very despair and confusion he feels when faced with the woman he has wronged that becomes the emotional springboard that catapults him from a state of inertia to one of restored and renewed ethical sensitivity and vision. He did not will this. It came about through a state of affairs which impinged on his consciousness and from which he could not escape. Of course, Nekhlyudov does take responsibility for what he has done, but the wellsprings of creativity are only tapped by him; he cannot recreate himself according to any rational understanding of the self he wishes to be. So we would wish to speak of taking responsibility for our ethical lives, but this not in the narrow sense of what Jung would call 'the ego-self' but in the widest sense where the self, grounded in the collective unconscious, is enabled to connect with positive archetypes that free the self to a greater self-understanding and enable ideas that have been repressed in the personal unconsciousness to emerge and realign, to enable the self to act in a deeper and more centred manner. That, again in Jungian terms, can be described as the journey towards consciousness and discrimination. It was the journey that Prince Nekhlyudov allowed himself to take, and it is a journey that we all need to embark upon if we are to discover the full extent of our human identity. And, like Nekhlyudov again, it may take a good stretch of a lifetime to work through.

The next two examples of resurrection each owe a significant debt to Judaism in the formulation of their ideas. This is a salutary reminder that the Christian faith was by no means revealed in one blinding flash to Paul on the Damascus road, but was an historical and synthetic development (some would call it 'heresy') of the faith of Israel based on the stories of the lives of Abraham, Isaac, Jacob and their successors. The idea of a general resurrection of the just was a late post-exilic idea developed mainly in Daniel and inter-testamental apocalyptic literature, as a compensation for the suffering and martyrdom experienced during the revolt of Judas Maccabeus against the imperial power. In this context, we can see how the microcosm crucifixion–resurrection in the story of Jesus is paralleled in the macrocosm by experiences of suffering and death leading to a triumph of the life-giving forces. Such a triumph does not always occur, of course, either in the text or in the world. The exiles to Babylon and Buchenwald remain painful and irreversible experiences of death. But the hope for the reemergence of new and life-giving meanings within desperate human situations is communicated by human stories told about the resurrection.

The English poet W. H. Auden (1907–73) rediscovered the Christian faith of his parents after meeting the young Jewish poet from Brooklyn, Chester Kallman, who was to remain his life-long companion. Although on his first visit to America, Auden was outside the immediate arena of warfare, he was acutely aware that the world situation could not have been much bleaker when he penned his momentous poem 'September 1, 1939':

> Defenceless under the night,
> Our world in stupor lies;
> Yet, dotted everywhere,
> Ironic points of light
> Flash out wherever the just
> Exchange their messages:
> May I, composed like them
> Of Eros and of dust,
> Beleaguered by the same
> Negation and despair,
> Show an affirming flame.[15]

Here there is one of the clearest modern interpretations of the Johannine insight that 'The light shineth in darkness; and the darkness comprehendeth it not'.[16] Despite the universal depression engendered by the thought of the imminent breakout of hostilities following Hitler's invasion of Poland, there were still good people who kept 'love and justice',[17] and in their negotiations the poet sees a model for living amidst the ever-present threat of horrific death. And Auden had a very vivid recollection, from his recent experience as a volunteer ambulance driver in the Spanish Civil War, of what some of those horrors could well portend. True to the Hebrew creation traditions, Auden realized his own human constitution, his frail frame, was made up of divine spark and mortal earth. The very word chosen for the species in the creation traditions, 'Adam', is a close cognate of the word for the clay of the soil (*adamah*). Midrashic tradition delightfully held that Adam, being divinely composed from soils from around the globe, was multi-coloured in his appearance. And the frailty that was aware of its mortality and of its guilt was at the same time the candleholder for an affirmation of the human spirit—best elicited in care or love for one's fellow creature. Kallman's personal contribution was that in taking Auden out of the prison of a loveless self, he reintroduced him to the wider human family and especially one that reached out to include the social outcasts—the non-Gentile, the homosexual, the stranger in the midst.[18]

In a chapter on 'Resurrection and the Body', Harry Williams argues that we can each as human beings experience the resurrection of the body even with the physical, emotional and sexual disabilities that each of us is prey to in differing degrees. We have to resist the danger of external stereotypes which tend to be imposed, which fail to take note of the personal standpoint of frailty and unrealized potential that each of us comes to at some particular stage on the journey of individuation:

> . . . or we shall be like a man dying of thirst by a mountain stream because there is no tap for him to turn on. *Eros*, with its roots deep in sexual feeling, can by acceptance be diffused throughout our entire physical structure so that every contact we have with others and the world we live in can be an act of physical love. It requires a miracle. But it is a miracle which has occurred to many men and women, and from which our disabilities in no way exclude us.'[19]

But more about this in the next chapter. For the moment we note that in Auden's poem the acceptance of self and other are mutually beneficial and parallel tasks. Neither of them comes easily to the individual self. To give up and despair often seems the more realistic assessment of the nightmare scenario in which one is found. Yet by fidelity to the genuine lights one sees one can 'show an affirming flame'. And a flame can set a city ablaze, or can be passed on as an Olympic torch. Although small and comparatively ordinary in itself, it has in front of it almost unlimited potentiality for heat and light. In the biblical witness, the metaphors of awakening, rising and enlightening are substantially interchangeable: 'Therefore it is said, "Awake, O sleeper, and arise from the dead, and Christ shall give you light".'[20] In a recent paper, Cupitt said of the need for preserving the meaning of such metaphors:

> We are looking for a religious vocabulary for today that will actually kindle people; and in these matters we invoke the metaphors of kindling and striking sparks by way of making the point that religious truth and faith depend upon a sudden flaring up of the imagination which can never quite be controlled or produced to order.[21]

This type of image is one that does not sit easily on the lips of conventional church people or those who wish to stress the bedrock or the traditions of their religious inheritance, since it is an image which allows elements of uncertainty to creep into their structure. Many religious people and their groupings prefer to keep the areas of uncertainty away, and to project them onto the secular world 'outside', while reassuring themselves of the bedrock of dogmas on which they believe they have constructed their own certainties. Although prepared to allow candles lit with due decorum in designated places in the churches, the idea of a living flame being kindled and passed on to others is an image less susceptible to control than it would seem comfortable for them in the present climate of economic and other uncertainties. The citadel does not require much light to function as a place of safety.

My final illustration of the contemporary meaning of the resurrection is a musical one. In involving both intellect and emotions through the world of sound, it is difficult if not impossible to write convincingly about its meaning, particularly when the example we have chosen is Gustav Mahler (1860–1911). Whenever I hear any of Mahler's ten symphonies, I feel by the end that I am drained both intellectually and emotionally. I seem to have been taken on a very long, tortuous journey that has stretched my senses to their limits. Wide overarching sweeps of emotion are made to carry poignant and careful questions posed by the composer's rigorous intellect. Mahler's Second Symphony is entitled 'Resurrection' and was inspired by the choral recitation of Klopstock's 'Resurrection Ode' at the funeral in Hamburg of the great pianist and conductor Hans von Bülow. Mahler said that when he heard it, 'it was as if I had been struck by lightning; everything suddenly rose before me clearly'. Mahler composed his symphony over a period of some six years, and after an immense labour the vast work (spanning 85 minutes, involving a choir, and an orchestra including ten horns, eight trumpets and much percussion) was first performed, conducted by Mahler, in Berlin in 1895.

He was pressed by his young friend Max Marchack to provide a dramatic programme to accompany the work. Mahler resisted this request at first, suggesting that it would be a false track to look for an event rather than a feeling in the work, but later he succumbed and spoke of the spiritual problem that lay behind this work. The problem was that of finding some assurance in the face of human mortality, and the resurrection provided some kind of reassurance in the presence of the overbearing suffering and essential fragility of the mortal estate.

The first movement of the Symphony ('Allegro Maestoso') he called the *Todtenfeier* ('Funeral Rites', 'Obsequies') and it deals with the great question:

Why do you live? Why did you suffer? Is it all nothing but a huge, frightful joke? We must answer these questions in some way, if we want to go on living—indeed, if we are to go on dying! He into whose life this call has once sounded must give an answer; and this answer I give in the final movement.[22]

Before we reach that, we have three interior movements of differing moods, the fourth of which is a simple, lightly orchestrated setting of the folk-poem 'Primal Light'. It encapsulates the deep religious longings of all in its searching words:

Man lies in deepest need,
Man lies in deepest pain,
Yes, rather would I be in heaven . .
I am from God and will return to God.

Into this voice of faith breaks in with a great crash the cry of disgust in the last movement:

We are confronted once more with terrifying questions. A voice is heard crying aloud: 'The end of all living things is come—the Last Judgement is at hand'. . . . The earth quakes, the graves burst open, the dead arise and stream on in endless procession. The great and the little ones of the earth—kings and beggars, righteous and godless—all press on; the cry for mercy and forgiveness strikes fearfully on our ears. . . . The last trumpet is heard—the trumpets of the Apocalypse ring out; in the eerie silence which follows, we can just catch the distant, barely audible song of a nightingale, a last tremulous echo of earthly life. A chorus of saints and heavenly beings softly breaks forth: 'Thou shalt arise, surely thou shalt arise.' Then appears the glory of God: a wondrous soft light penetrates us to the heart—all is holy calm. And behold, it is no judgement;

there are no sinners, no just. None is great, none small.
There is no punishment and no reward. An overwhelming
love illuminates our being. We know and are.[23]

Within this programme that Mahler has provided we glimpse
much of traditional Judaeo-Christian eschatological language,
about the last things, coupled with a vision of a most radical
novelty. The tradition of judgement and division becomes dis-
placed by the superior understanding of a love that affirms us
and knows us not for some future event but in the immediacy
of our *now*. Here Mahler reveals his identity as an existential
composer of our times, one who has encapsulated (to use the
title of David Holbrook's theological study of his works) 'the
courage to be'[24]—which is a very contemporary understanding
of courage. At the same time we must take some caution before
we enlist Mahler in the Sea of Faith Network, as he later
recanted from this detailed programme of his work, writing to
his wife: that 'In fact, as religious doctrines do, it leads directly
to a flattening and coarsening, and in the long run to such
distortion that the work . . . is utterly unrecognizable'.[25] Such
a distortion can also be argued to be behind much of the
misunderstanding of Christian doctrine that seems to have happened within the ongoing institution of the church and its theological interpretations. In his study on the resurrection, Harry
Williams has argued that from early on in its history Christianity followed the pattern of most religions in substituting
knowledge as possession for knowledge as communion. From
AD 180 when Irenaeus described the church as a 'truth bank',
the church has also tended to focus not so much on the insights
of Jesus as on its own claims to be the repository of truth:

> The churches, if they are to lead men to what gives them
> life, cannot evade the necessity of death and resurrection
> in this sphere as in all others. They must be prepared to
> die to the claim that they possess the truth in their

doctrinal conceptualizations, in order to be roused up as witnesses to mystery which can be known only by means of knowledge as communion.[26]

The theme of this symphony is undoubtedly related strongly to the *Leitmotif* which runs throughout Mahler's work—namely, the challenge to find some significance in a life which is doomed to extinction. But the quest for meaning is here orchestrated with a refinement and a complexity that is beyond either my powers or the scope of this chapter to analyse. Suffice it to say that the symphony was a product of someone whose experience has been indelibly seared by suffering and death (including that of his own daughter as a child) and who pines for a convincing and a reassuring resolution to 'the agony and the ecstasy' which has been his lot.

Before moving on, it might be helpful to see if anything remains consistent in the four contemporary portrayals of resurrection we have exemplified. Different though each of them are, there are some common themes that are worth comment. The first and most obvious point is the particularity of the settings and the experiences described, at least in the literary works, whether it be the village of Cookham with its quaint but delightful characters, Imperial Russia with its splendour and bureaucracy, or cosmopolitan New York at the outbreak of World War Two. Nothing in the text links these particular places and times with any other place, or any other time. Only in the cultural setting of its time and placing can any experience of resurrection be perceived as a resolution. We cannot transpose the solutions of those in one cultural setting and hand them down, as if 'ready-made', on a plate to those in another. This is the mistake which Leonard Hodgson described as to 'assume that someone somewhere, at some time in the past, really knew the truth and that what we have to do is to find out what he thought and get back to it'.[27] This has been a particular problem for those who have wished any authentic experience of resurrection to be linked explicitly to the biblical witness. The assumption has been that only if sufficient links are made with the biblical material will any experience be deemed to be an authentic experience of resurrection. But the biblical writers had different experiences from our own, and it is by no means clear that there are even common features in their separate accounts and understandings of resurrection such as we have exemplified in the gospels. So it would seem not only unnecessary but also very difficult to maintain any essential link as necessary for salvation.

Another important feature of these examples is that the 'raising up' is not located on any temporal sequence as a later or even as a last event in a series, which has to include the earlier steps of suffering and death. In Spencer's work the resurrection is clearly an event in time; it is into the midst of Nekhlyudov's emotional turmoil that the new light on his situation breaks in; Auden wishes to do his affirmation of others in the foreboding situation he and they find themselves to be in; and in Mahler's great work the pendulum forever swings between the ominous fearful sections in which life appears senseless and futile and the sections in which meaning appears to be offered the soul and harmony is perceived as not only possible but delightful. The meaning of the resurrection is not to be located 'on the third day', in the sense of 'on the far side' of suffering; but within the texture of suffering it is a joyful, visible and triumphant strand. This is a truth glimpsed in the Fourth Gospel when Jesus is credited with the prophecy, 'I, when I am lifted up from the earth, will draw all men to myself'.[28] The crucifixion and resurrection are not separate events. They are two conceptions of the same event, the being-lifted-up which the cross entailed. In our time no writer has better expressed this intricate connection than the French writer Simone Weil who experienced great suffering in a short life but showed in her writings how it could be transformed through a kind of 'mysticism of attention':

> The joy of Easter is not that which follows upon suffering,
> freedom after the chains, satiety after hunger, reunion
> after separation. It is joy which lies beyond suffering and
> achievement. Suffering and joy are in perfect balance.
> Suffering is the opposite of joy; but joy is not the opposite
> of suffering.[29]

If joy is often to be found in the midst of suffering then we
must remember that there is no suffering in abstract. As Gustav
Mahler suffered a very real sense of individual abandonment
connected to the Judaism that was his own tradition, so Beet-
hoven wrestled with his increasing deafness, and Tchaikovsky
with his sexual anxieties. Each had the task of forging a music
that emerged triumphant out of his particular trial. And that
is the type of creativity we are each called to, as we each work
out who we are and what are our individual tasks. Often a link
between perceived weakness and potential strength will emerge,
but there is no easy equation or formula. The struggle will often
be fierce and life-long. But the final clue I would suggest we
can find in each of the examples I have given is the quality of
'attention', 'waiting', or what Simone Weil has characterized as
'attentiveness'. By accepting the situation (whatever it may be)
and delving into its depths, we may encounter the risen life
within. Hence Spencer's characters are primarily alert and
watchful as they stand up and peer from their graves. Nekhlyudov and Auden speak an unspoken prayer that they may be
more alerted to the needs of others than hitherto in their lives;
Mahler's music incites us to examine our pain and perplexity
in the light of a deeper harmony which is not apart but resounds
underneath. We may be reminded of Auden's paradox of
creativity:

> The slight despair at what we are,
> The marginal grief,
> Is the source of life.

At the end of his book on the resurrection, Harry Williams suggests that with regard to the afterlife, the pessimistic and rationalistic will tend to deny, while the optimistic and romantic to affirm its existence. He believes we can retain traditional imagery as long as we make distinctions between 'hope' and 'desire'.[30] My feeling is that the earliest biblical accounts of resurrection faith were not in essence eschatological but always realized. Or in simpler terms, to believe in eternal life was ever meant to be an insight into this life rather than any glimpse into the next. Since Christianity *par excellence* among the religions calls us to deny the self, any attempt to rehabilitate the self in another world ought to be resisted as a form of selfishness.

Why do religious people so need to cling to their terminology for a reality that they are the first to say is not of their creation? Surely it is more vital to be in touch with the wellsprings of spiritual life than it is to chant the right words? There seems to be a fear abroad that if we leave go of the traditional words we become loosed from our sense of meaning. The truth is rather that we can become empowered to use those words again, in a resurrected sense, in different combinations and patterns, to re-create our own patterns of meaning. For most people this is too daunting a task; better to retreat into past and loved formulations. But a retreat such as this is a choice to live only on the surface, and a surface living denies the possibility of a real tapping of the wellsprings which rise up from the deepest recesses. The religious task is surely to open up the links between language and depth and to challenge people to live both deeply and creatively in the divine image, for ever being renewed and having former dreams replaced by newer and more challenging visions for their time.

Much use has been made in this chapter of the metaphor of light in darkness. I would like to conclude this consideration of how a non-realist would regard the doctrine of the resurrection with a contrast between two pictures entitled *The Light of the World*—each of which adorns a college chapel. The first, by

William Holman Hunt, hanging in the Gothic chapel of Keble College, Oxford, illustrates the words of the risen Christ, 'Behold, I stand at the door and knock; if any one hears my voice and opens the door, I will come in to him and eat with him, and he with me'.[31] A bearded Jesus in a cope, bedecked with crown of thorns, knocks at the door of the human sinner and awaits any possible response. Outside in the wood it is dark indeed, but Jesus carries a bright oil lantern to bring light to the believer inside. The gaze of Jesus looks out from the canvas into our own eyes for a response. However, a realistic vision of Jesus elicits only a contemporary response of quaintness, and the work leaves us cold as before a period piece. By contrast, John Piper's illustration of the window in Robinson College, Cambridge, sheds on those who glimpse it a light for our post-modern day. There is no figure at all in this illustration, only a chiaroscuro of colour. At the foot of the window is the dark green of foliage which builds up to the blues and reds of sky and sun. It is a radiant vision of the natural world, made radiant by the transforming light of the sun. This is a non-realist resurrection. Probably it speaks to fewer people—the chapel seats 30 as opposed to Keble's 500—but the contemporaneity of the vision speaks to our time in a way that only a contemporary artist could portray. We admire an older, more traditional view of the resurrection but it cannot convict us with the same force as it could Holman Hunt's nineteenth-century contemporaries. In the century that has elapsed in between these works of art much has been questioned and much of our understanding of the gospel has changed. Only a portrait of the resurrection which faces up to that change and takes it on board will be one that will evince a response in the world in which we find ourselves living towards the end of the twentieth century.

Notes

1 Don Cupitt, speaking at the University of East Anglia, 15 May 1985.

2 Quoted by Professor Robin Butlin in his introduction to the eighth Annual

Chaplaincy Lecture at Loughborough University, *The Future of Christianity in the West*.

3 David Strauss, *Life of Jesus* (Chapman Bros, 1846), and cf. his biography by Horton Harris, *David Friedrich Strauss and His Theology* (Cambridge University Press, 1972).

4 Rudolf Bultmann, 'New Testament and mythology' in *Kerygma and Myth: A Theological Debate* (SPCK, 1972), vol. 1, p. 42.

5 John Macquarrie, *Principles of Christian Theology* (SCM, 1966), pp. 265f.

6 *Doctrine in the Church of England* (first published 1938; SPCK, 1957), p. 86, appended note.

7 Quoted in an article by the Religious Affairs Correspondent, Walter Schwarz, 'Carey casts doubt on physical nature of Christ's resurrection', *The Guardian* (9 May 1992).

8 Quoted in the epigraph of the novel by Albert Camus, *The Myth of Sisyphus* (Penguin, 1975).

9 Prayers from *The Alternative Service Book 1980*, pp. 308, 314, 317 (my emphasis).

10 George Herbert, 'Prayer (I)' in *The Works of George Herbert*, ed. F. E. Hutchinson (Oxford University Press, 1941), quoted in and providing the title for Nicholas Lash's *Easter in Ordinary* (SCM, 1988), p. 295.

11 Quoted by George Pattison in *Art, Modernity and Faith* (Macmillan, 1991), p. 6.

12 Leo Tolstoy, *Resurrection*, trans. Louise Maude (Grosset & Dunlap, 1899), p. 2.

13 Ibid., p. 519.

14 John 20.19.

15 W. H. Auden, *Collected Shorter Poems 1930–1944* (Faber & Faber, 1950), p. 76.

16 John 1.5 (Authorised Version).

17 Hosea 12.6.

18 Cf. here the work by Chester Kallman's mother, Dorothy J. Farnan, *Auden in Love* (Faber & Faber, 1984).

19 H. A. Williams, *True Resurrection* (Fount, 1983), p. 57.

20 Ephesians 5.14.

21 Don Cupitt, 'Non-Realism and God', a paper delivered at the Sea of Faith V Conference (1992).

22 Gustav Mahler, quoted in Deryck Cooke, *Gustav Mahler: An Introduction to his Music* (Faber & Faber, 1980), p. 53.

23 Ibid., p. 53–4.

24 David Holbrook, *Gustav Mahler and the Courage to Be* (Vision Press, 1975).

25 Gustav Mahler, quoted in Cooke, *Gustav Mahler*, p. 54.

26 Williams, *True Resurrection*, p. 99.

27 Quoted in Dennis Nineham, *Christian Believing: Report by the Doctrine Commission of the Church of England* (SPCK, 1976), p. 87.

28 John 12.32.

29 Simone Weil, *First and Last Notebooks* (Oxford University Press, 1970), p. 69.

30 Williams, *True Resurrection*, p. 179.

31 Revelation 3.20.

3 The body

Man or woman, I might tell you how I like you, but cannot,
And might tell what's in me and what is in you, but cannot,
And might tell that pining I have, that pulse of my nights
   and days.
Behold, I do not give lectures or a little charity,
When I give, I give myself.[1]

For too long the body has been imprisoned in the Real world.
From the time of Plato through into the era ruled by the Real
God of Judaeo-Christianity, the body has been placed in a
universal hierarchy of values in the West. This hierarchy has
kept it firmly in submission to higher 'spiritual' powers and
laws, and the price of acceptance of the body has been its
unquestioning subjection to their authority. In the dualistic
theology we have all inherited within that tradition an unquestioned priority was given to the 'spiritual' over the 'physical',
and again to the 'masculine' over the 'feminine'.

In a splendid summary of the history of sexuality within the
Christian tradition, the writer Philip Sherrard has summed up
the mood of the centuries:

> Sexuality is tainted. . . . If not actually evil in itself, its use
> stirs up the passions and so leads directly to sin. It is the
> springhead through which the tribes of evil pour into
> human nature. Consequently, any progress in the life of
> the spirit demands as an initial step the circumventing or
> transcending of sexuality.[2]

Sherrard goes on to document how such a general negative
understanding of the body and interpersonal relationships per-

vades the Christian traditions of both West and East. Nevertheless, he goes on to show how the Eastern tradition has had
insights into the dynamics of sexuality which have been neglected in the West to its peril. While the Western tradition followed
Augustine's emphasis on the sexual act itself as the basis of
sexual differentiation, and developed subsequently a highly
legalistic code distinguishing which acts were legal and in what
context, the Eastern tradition has been much more ready to
evaluate the sexual element in our make-up as part of our very
nature as human beings, and therefore has concentrated on
questions of identity rather than specific acts. So the nineteenth-
century Russian writer Nicholas Berdyaev (1874–1948) wrote:

> Man's sexual nature cannot be placed on the same level
> with other functions of his organism, even the most
> essential, such as the circulation of the blood. In man's
> sexuality we perceive the metaphysical roots of his
> being. . . . We cannot escape from sex. We may leave aside
> the differentiated function of sex, we may deny or conquer
> this 'natural' function. But in this case man's sexual
> function is only transferred—and man still remains a
> sexual being.[3]

He goes on to point out how the Greeks knew that Hades
and Dionysus were the same god; they realized the mystical
connection that tied together aspects of death and sexuality, so
that sexual feeling itself contained an element which he referred
to as 'a deathly anguish'.

In his book on *Existentialism* Professor John Macquarrie, in a
chapter entitled 'The body and the Other, with special reference
to sexuality', reminds us of the metaphysical aspects of our
sexual constitution. In the 'ecstasy' of sexual encounter, he
argues, we have literally the 'standing out' of the self in a unity
of being-with-the-Other:

In a discussion of Henry Miller, Arthur Gibson (in *The Faith of an Atheist*) has made the point that, 'The mystery of sex is the mystery of total contact between created existents.' Sex is thus an attempt at a total sharing of being. If Berdyaev is right (as I believe he is) in insisting that human sexuality is not just a biological function but has its inescapable ontological dimension, then even so-called 'casual' acts of sex cannot be regarded as merely peripheral to existence but are bound to affect the persons concerned quite deeply; for in them too something of the totality of being-with-the-Other is expressed, however badly.[4]

So sexuality, defined fairly widely in terms of our being-with-others, thus takes on a metaphysical dimension. It reveals to us as humans an ineradicable part of our identity. Our destiny is to be in relationship with others; to speak of relationship it is necessary to speak about sexuality. Jack Dominian, in his important book *The Church and the Sexual Revolution*, added an important aspect to this contributed by psychoanalysis:

Until this century sexuality was described in adult terms of primarily heterosexual attraction, leading to intercourse and procreation. Thus the emphasis was on heterosexuality, coitus, erotic pleasure and fertility, all of which tended to emphasise the biologically active post-pubertal features of sexuality. One genius changed all this. Sigmund Freud dropped his bombshell in 1905 with his *Three Essays on the Theory of Sexuality*.[5]

Freud has shown us how that mode of being involves our sexuality from our very earliest relationship with our parents, and that much of our adult sexual history is a recapitulation of much of that earlier dynamic.

One of the components in the 'anguish' involved in questions of sexual identity has been the problem of establishing the context in which the explicitly sexual expression of relationships should take place. Whereas the West has traditionally defined sexual expression as permissible only within the confines of a legally binding institution called marriage, the Russians have always regarded a profound and serious bond between men and women based on true love as having the status of marriage regardless of state or ecclesiastical legalities. Clearly these are different cultural understandings of what marriage is.

And of course the confinement of sexual expression to the bonds of marriage has anyhow been seriously challenged. One of the problems has been the contemporary questioning of the 'male'/'female' gender-differentiation, which may not speak so clearly to individual 'gender'-identity as it does to biological differentiation. Both East and West have discovered in recent times that elements of masculine and feminine sexuality are present in *each* gender. So here Berdyaev argued:

> The world-differentiation into male and female can never
> finally wipe out the basic genuine bisexuality, the
> androgynous quality in man—the image and likeness of
> God in him. In truth neither man nor woman is the image
> and likeness of God but only the androgyne—the youth/
> maiden, the integral bisexual man.

In Berdyaev's understanding, the gender distinction as we know it was a result of the fall of Adam and therefore is essentially an alien polarization we need to transcend if we are to be redeemed from the fallen state of existence.[6] So, his argument seemed to imply, the rediscovery of an original bisexuality was a necessary part of human redemption, in the individual as in the race. It was at the Fall that the Virgin Isophia was separated from Adam and withdrawn into the heavens, where she was replaced by the earthly Eve, the woman of this world. Through relationship with her, Adam had the potential either

to bind himself to the principle of animal sexuality and generation, or to become reintegrated into the androgynous source of
his nature by rediscovering the Eternal Female within the
earthly woman.

Whereas this Eastern imagery is highly dualist and metaphor-
ical, the Western world has produced a much more rationalist
and 'scientific' critique of the same traditional gender-
definitions. So, in his book *The Interpersonal Theory of Psychiatry*,
the American psychoanalyst Harry Stack Sullivan argued that
any relationship established between two people could be classi-
fied into three types of intimacy (autophilic, isophilic, hetero-
philic), four types of interpersonal objective (auto-, homo-,
hetero-, kata-sexual) and six types of genital definition (ortho-,
para-, meta-, amphi-, mutual masturbation, and onanism),
resulting in 72 theoretical patterns of sexual behaviour between
any two people in relationship.

In a comment on this classification into these two types, the
Catholic writer Donald Goergen comments (and his comment
may receive more general assent than Sullivan's precise classification):

> From this statement, I would like you to realize, if you
> realize nothing else, how fatuous it is to toss out the
> adjectives 'hetero', 'homo' or 'narcisstic' to classify a person
> as to his sexual and friendly integrations with others.
> Such classifications are not anywhere near refined enough
> for intelligent thought; they are much too gross to do
> anything except mislead both the observer and the victim.
> For example, to talk about homosexuality's being a
> problem really means about as much as about humanity's
> being a problem.[7]

Without a real God, there is no universal hierarchy and
equally no fixed personal sexual identity. Rather than accepting
the idea gaining increasing pseudo-scientific credence that

sexual orientation and degree of sexual drive are always some-thing genetically inherited and being fixed before birth, a non-realist modern understanding of sexual identity would accept the view that all personal relationships have an erotic element which can then be particularized and intensified in some chosen relationships. We are free to make responsible choices about those with whom we wish a greater degree of explicitly sexual participation, and we are also, of course, freer to decide in what form of sexual communication we wish to participate than has been traditionally recognized, or at least admitted, in Judaeo-Christian society. For example, the advent of AIDS has led us to realize that penetrative sex is only one option among several forms of active interpersonal engagement with a partner. Freely chosen celibacy is another option which is more acceptable now than it was deemed twenty years ago, and cannot only be chosen but also affirmed – but only on the renewed understand-ing that celibacy no more eliminates affective sexual feeling between individuals than any other form of sexual lifestyle. Indeed, it may even enhance it!

We have also come to learn that, in taking full human respon-sibility for the choices we make as individuals in this area of our lives, we are members of a society that has formed us, and different societies have exercised different pressures to conform sexually. Who can say that polygamous marriage, common in parts of Africa, is wrong because we do not practise it in the West? In societies in which women are more undervalued than our own, who is to rule that this is not a more generally careful form of providing for them? Similarly, who is to rule that promiscuous homosexuality in our own culture is not a more liberating style of living for those who choose to engage in it than that of those who cut the possibility of homosexual feeling out of their emotional lives and oppose its expression wherever they find it in others?

Such tricky questions lead people of any faith and none to seek authoritative answers from whatever tradition will dispel personal doubts. But if no such authoritative answers exist, then every formulation must certainly be questioned and choices made as much on 'tried and tested' grounds as on any other.

So, when we look at the institution of marriage as conceived by the Established church in this country, we observe a great longing for traditionalism and for a realist understanding of the contract even when the background belief in an ordering/permitting deity has fallen into abeyance. Again, I would turn to my experience as an inner-city parish priest where it appeared the less people seemed to want to give any credence to a transcendent deity, the more they wanted to hold that in a marriage ceremony in a traditional church a real alteration to their personal relationship effected by the priest would somehow produce a more substantial bond than that which had existed heretofore in the relationship. And perhaps it did, although more probably because of perceived expectations than any sacramental understanding of what the ceremony 'did' to the couple who were making the vows. In this regard, although the traditional white wedding in church may well have become more popular now than at any previous stage in British history, it does not produce any more guarantees of longevity. If anything, quite the opposite. As more divorcees are allowed to remarry in Anglican churches, so the demand increases. And with regard to the institution of marriage at large, the point made at the start of the so-called 'Permissive Decade' by Don Cupitt's predecessor as Dean of Emmanuel College, Cambridge is still very much to the point:

> Against the permanent god-givenness of marriage we have
> Christ's words that in his father's kingdom there was
> neither marriage nor giving in marriage—there is at least
> (here) the suggestion that marriage was instituted
> amongst men [*sic*] in accordance with their needs and
> powers at particular times and places.[8]

In a recent discussion with my multi-racial congregation in the University concerning a marriage I was about to bless between two research students, a Zimbabwean made the suggestion that in his culture the girl in question would have commanded a much higher dowry than usual because of her attainment of a Loughborough PhD. This caused wry surprise on the part of her intended groom, since in his understandably Western calculation of the benefits of marriage, his fiancée's academic credentials had not featured in any conscious calculation. Equally, there were elements of the Western arrangement (such as the relative lack of interest in the choice of a partner by the respective families of the students, and the existence of a detailed wedding-present list prepared and carefully monitored by the bride's mother) which caused equal surprise and amusement on the part of the Zimbabwean. It would seem that elements regarded as essential in one cultural understanding of marriage had been trivialized or were even non-existent in another.

Within Western society itself, the development in our understanding of the role of women has challenged the concept of dependence in different degrees. While in some churches the most radical choice the couple have to make with their officiating minister is whether or not the bride is going to promise 'to obey' and the groom 'to worship', in others even the imagery of the father walking up the aisle with his daughter and 'giving her away' has been substituted as an outmoded conception of what is going on.[9] Is there an essential component of marriage without which it cannot be said to be a marriage at all? It is difficult to see what, if anything, that element could be. Would it be the exchange of vows? But they seem to be infinitely re-writeable. Is it the life-commitment? But that has been dispensed with in some ceremonies. Is it the complementarity of the sexes? But homosexual marriages have been performed in various churches and states. So this would suggest that marriage is an infinitely malleable form of agreed contract that is continually being modified and refined, carrying no more intrinsic value or authority than any other form of commitment that human beings may decide to take upon themselves within their society.

Within our society in the West we can observe a number of modifications that have developed over the past generation or two in our general understanding of marriage. One of the most important trends would be the movement from seeing marriage as the effective beginning of a living together to an understanding of it more as a step of further or deeper commitment by the individuals involved. So cohabitation of partners before they take their vows has become more of a norm. In Britain, this prompted the July 1992 meeting of the General Synod of the Church of England in York to call upon the bishops to study the phenomenon rather than to condemn it out of hand. The model for seeing marriage in this way as the last and most public of a chain of developing commitments is already provided by the Afro-Caribbean community, a community loosely scattered through Britain and North America, traditionally Christian, and one in which the solemnization of marriage vows often takes place when children of the partnership are well on the path to their teenage years. Despite this, the relationships entered into are remarkably strong and faithful, and do not appear to require the legal form of marriage to shore them up.

Since this earlier stage of mutual commitment, that of 'engagement' or 'betrothal', has become almost a necessary precursor to marriage in large sections of our society, churchmen have proposed a liturgical context of betrothal which would be a serious commitment by the individuals concerned but without the binding legal and life commitments required by the Marriage Service. Bishop John Spong refers to this suggestion made earlier by former Archbishop of Canterbury Geoffrey Fisher, and he himself calls it 'an idea whose time has come'.[10]

We should note just how radical a departure this proposal (as others in this area) would be. It is important to notice that this suggestion is not one of reviving a biblical or traditional idea at all. It is true that the biblical account seems to include concepts of betrothal that would allow for intimacy within the commitment. But the proposal for a public and liturgical ceremony of commitment, Spong argues, could not have been made a century ago.[11] It is proposed as a response to changing social conditions, by which the advances in Western education have now raised the average age of marriage to the mid-twenties whilst the development of puberty has become equally significantly earlier. There is, in consequence, now a greater gap between the time when an individual can fully function sexually and the time that he or she is expected to marry than has ever been the case before. Different cultures and epochs require different, and newly conceived, religious responses to their developing needs, and here is a case in point where society needs to 'invent' an appropriate means of public expression of a commonly perceived social reality. Until such a form of words is available, there will inevitably be a large 'grey' area of hypocrisy and play-acting where people are forced to uphold the existing institution whilst admitting privately that it does not fulfil perceived needs. Such a mode of existence is well illustrated by the playwright David Hare in his witty and perceptive insight into the contemporary Church of England, *Racing Demon*. The enthusiastic young evangelical curate Tony Ferris speaks to his fiancée Frances Parnell about the unease he feels about their long-lasting sexual relationship:

> I have been getting worried how it may look to the rest of the world. I mean, you know I don't have any hang-ups. Personally. The biblical evidence is pretty inconclusive. We all know. We have advanced. Paul wasn't Jesus. You can read the bible either way. All that so-called Christian morality, we understand it can be too narrowly interpreted. It's a question of what feels right in your heart. And with you it's always felt right. I promise you. I

believe in the expression of God's love through another human being. In a serious context, it's good.[12]

Pulled in one direction by a realist view of biblical ethics and in another by the truth of his own experience, Tony does not know how to respond to the dilemma in which he finds himself, and his dithering in a moral maze effectively nudges Frances into breaking off their relationship. A realistic theology which Tony has freely espoused has failed to provide him with any adequate tools with which he can solve his sexual dilemma — here that a relationship very important to his life is none the less (in being sexually intimate) one condemned by the type of theology he believes himself called to impart. A non-realist would here, as in so many other contemporary ethical situations, be so much better equipped to see his or her way through. For he or she would realize that there is no absolute format of relationship between any two people with which we have to try and comply as individuals in relationship. In Tony's case, the sudden tragic death of his parents in a car crash brought Frances close to him at the time when, being stretched in his training for ministry, he needed a strong caring relationship.

Tony had been ordained and had recently started his first job as an inner-city curate. Inevitably such a dramatic change in his circumstances brings into question the nature and future of this relationship. How Tony envisages the relationship with Frances in his new role and setting is in fact *the* challenge to the relationship at this point. Any decision about the future of his relationship with Frances revolves entirely around the situation in which she and he find themselves. The connection with the Bible or any other external authority is neither a helpful nor a harmful factor since it does not exist. It is an irrelevance, and if the Bible or other 'authorities' are cited, then they are being cited as a 'cover' rather than being relevant documentation that could be applied to the circumstances. It has to be freely admitted that, in the words of a respected contemporary New Testament scholar, biblical ethics in this area are pre-scientific and at best naïve.[13] If this is the case, then to cite the Bible as authoritative in itself can be a danger and unhelpful because it can appear to be simply authoritarian. On the other hand, when we are prepared to read the biblical writers as human beings attempting to wrestle with their own very primitive ideas about sexual relationships and their dynamics (rather than as commandments issued by God), we may then be freed to take the courage of our own responsibility for our deep relationships and handle them with a sensitivity informed by the findings of twentieth-century psychoanalysis and social studies, which will help us to discern how they become formed within our individual psyches and what may be the reasonable course of their future development. And by doing this we can take a handle on the deep relationships we are each of us engaged in by virtue of being members of a human society, whether those relationships become explicitly sexual or are only potentially so. Passing through the degrees of sexual intimacy, in all our varying friendships and loves, can become an exercise of learning that we perform more consciously now that we have discovered just how deep and wide the potential of our human relationships is.

As we have warned previously, liberal theology in the past may have been rather too sanguine in this area as much as in others, in its promise that by embracing the insights of the contemporary culture we may find a positive and clear solution to human dilemmas.[14] It may well be much more difficult than we have thought.

Let us take the example of homosexuality and its practice. Here as elsewhere it might appear to be the easiest course to replace a negative realistic stance with a more positive one. So, for example, if we no longer believe the claim made by Herbert Waddams in the (then standard) *New Introduction to Moral Theology*, written from the Anglican perspective in 1964, that

'Those who indulge in homosexual activities . . . commit an offence against God and against society',[15] then we must still decide what we do believe about homosexual activities and on what grounds. Some would claim that a 'gay' society ought to mirror 'straight' society and that gay 'marriages' should be offered as part of the social choice. While a non-realist would not want to deny this as an option, he or she would want to reiterate the point already made at the beginning of this chapter that, in the words of Spong, 'Christianity, if it is to engage the future, [must] rid itself of all its defining sexual stereotypes'.[16] While some homosexuals may discover a partner with whom they wish to spend the rest of their lives in a commitment parallel to that of heterosexual marriage, their particular choice must not become the only permitted format for being homosexual. If it were to be allowed to do that, then what would that tell us all that would help the erotic feelings which are universal and which the Quakers in their 1963 Report called 'the homosexual in each one of us [that] helps us in handling our own sex'?[17] Part of the problem we all have is a homophobia that emerges from our cultural conditioning to condemn those feelings as they arise within us. We need to be given knowledge and resources to handle those feelings positively, and if the *Kinsey Report* (1957) and other reports on contemporary sexual practice are right, then individuals in the course of their lives change their position on the heterosexual–homosexual spectrum. If that is the case, then a life-long commitment, or a definition of an individual as 'gay', may well be not only unrealistic but unhelpful to the relationship or to the individual concerned. Teenage friendships, casual sexual encounters for profit, the friendship of an older for a younger person; the forms of homosexuality in its affective expression are so diverse that at least one recent Christian commentator has suggested it might be more helpful to think along the lines of the Heinz company with their '57 varieties' rather than of a monochrome psychological type, to think of homosexualities rather than homosexuality.[18] And, of course, a non-realist would want to point out that it should not continually be prefixed in moral jargon by the 'problem of . . .', since there is no one problem, or challenge, but many, which are perceived only in the articulation of what particular problems and challenges arrive in relationship to one's own sex.

In some areas in our society, the non-realist interpretation is gaining ground here. For example, in the investigation and treatment of HIV/AIDS, the medical world has moved significantly in the past three years from talking of 'risk groups' (such as drug-abusers and male homosexuals) to 'risk activities' (such as penetrative and homosexual anal sex) since it is believed that such language provides a more accurate handle on the ways in which people actually conduct their personal lives, acting as they freely choose in the situations they find themselves in, rather than by conforming to social stereotypes of who they allegedly are.

To conclude: a non-realist admits to no intrinsic sacred connection linking the self to a universal or higher self called 'God'. The human self is revealed primarily in our experience of others' identity and of our own. Our understanding of our own self-identity inevitably includes a corporeal element. We do not 'possess' a body (that is the old Realist language implying the superiority of the mind) but our experience of self and others inevitably includes our bodily experience. That experience is extremely malleable and depends a lot on our formative experiences in childhood, and also on the perceptions we place on our world. So, for example, a child frequently sexually abused will grow up with a markedly different attitude to adults from a child who has been entirely deprived of human company. In each case, there may be considerable apprehension of the sexual element in adult relationships, but that apprehension will reveal itself differently—in both verbal and non-verbal communications. Equally, the social projects with which we become involved reflect the common understanding of those with whom we have chosen to share our particular visions. So the language and the activities of a drug-abusing squat will present a markedly different view of their external world to a group of religious committed to relief of the poor. We do not need to make value-judgements here, but we do have to realize at the outset that if religion is conceived as the creation of value-structures by individuals, then the complexity of corporeal relationships in developed societies inevitably inclines to complex rather than simplistic definitions of our society or community. Also, as individuals, we inhabit overlapping worlds of meaning which increase the complexity further. I may find myself a fan of a particular sports team, an adherent of a particular religious denomination, a member of a special profession, a party member and a keen instrumentalist participating in a specialized type of music-making. My life does not make in this case for straight choices. I may also find that I alone am in a position of being a member simultaneously of each and every of these several human groupings. It is an unenviable position that no one can truly appreciate 'from the inside' the particular combination and clash of interests that such a plural membership entails. The point is that I am responsible for the meaning of what others know as my identity and only by exercising my own choices in the conflicts I experience will I assert to others my own concept of the self I am choosing to develop.

It may have been noticed in this conclusion that we have passed beyond the narrow conception of the body as a sexual being. But from the outset a non-realist account of the body has anticipated the objection. By experiencing the others simultaneously with the self, we experience a necessary sexuality. But our body is not defined by our gender nor are we driven entirely by our sexual drives. Existence with others can become as explicitly erotic as we wish to make it, or it can take the form of a meeting which cannot be usefully explained by our sexual language. Once again, the choice is our own, as a society that to a certain extent participates in a common linguistic understanding—explicitly sexual today, not at all in Victorian Britain—and as individuals who take responsibility for the form of our converse with others, and within the limitations of our own society know how to inhabit and present our own bodily selves in the image, not of God, but of the identity we wish to project at this particular stage of a developing process. 'Love your neighbour as yourself' or 'Hell is other people' take meaning as they are chosen by us as our means of expression. In our efforts to dismantle all overbearing Real models, we can lay hold of an understanding which releases us as individuals freely able to create the persons we want to be, in our bodies and in our world of bodies.

Notes

1 Walt Whitman, *Song of Myself*, lines 991–5.

2 Philip Sherrard, *Christianity and Eros* (SPCK, 1976), p. 5.

3 Nicholas Berdyaev, *The Meaning of the Creative Act* (Harper, 1955), pp. 18off.

4 Professor John Macquarrie, *Existentialism* (Penguin, 1976), p. 116; Cf. Arthur Gibson, *The Faith of an Atheist* (Harper & Row, 1968).

5 Jack Dominian, *The Church and the Sexual Revolution* (Darton, Longman & Todd, 1971), p. 17.

6 Berdyaev, *The Meaning of the Creative Act*, pp. 18off.

7 Harry Stack Sullivan, quoted in Donald Goergen, *The Sexual Celibate* (SPCK, 1976), p. 83.

8 Howard E. Root, 'Ethical problems of sex', *Theology* (October 1962).

9 Bishop John Shelby Spong of Newark has described how he refused to give any of his five daughters away, and has written on this subject extensively in *Living in Sin?* (Harper, 1990); cf. esp. pp. 54–66.

10 Cf. Spong, *Living in Sin?*, pp. 177–87.

11 Ibid., p. 179.

12 David Hare, *Racing Demon* (Faber & Faber, 1990), p. 8.

13 Rev. Professor Leslie Houlden, in correspondence with the author.

14 Cf. Chapter 1, p. 22.

15 Herbert Waddams, *A New Introduction to Moral Theology* (SCM, 1964), p. 145.

16 John Shelby Spong, *The Future of Christianity in the West* (Loughborough University, 1992), p. 12.

17 *Towards a Quaker View of Sex* (Friends' House Service Committee, 1963), p. 19.

18 Canon Eric James, in conversation with the author. Cf. Eric James, *The Challenge of Sexual Prejudice* (Loughborough University, 1991).

4 How and what do non-realists worship?

Anselm prayed in all inwardness that he might succeed in proving God's existence. He thinks he has succeeded, and he flings himself down in adoration to thank God. Amazing. He does not notice that this prayer and this expression of thanksgiving are infinitely more proof of God's existence than the proof.[1]

Traditional language about God has concentrated as much on worship as on doctrine. Following Anselm's definition of God as 'that than which nothing greater can be thought', it was held that the highest object of human contemplation was of necessity worthy also of the greatest human devotion. And since humankind is primarily a linguistic animal, from the beginning language was an important component of that worship, alongside music and symbolic action. So traditional theology has accompanied traditional 'liturgy' (a Greek word connoting 'devotion' or 'service') in worship of a real God. Indeed, one strand in Christian theology has always regarded the work of doctrine as secondary to the work of the liturgy and subservient to it. In this understanding, theologians have the task not of enquiring into the nature of God so much as providing the believers with formulae of worship which aim for the most sublime poetry and highest conceptual refinement. In this understanding, worship is humankind's highest and most worthy calling; the articulation of one's belief is secondary to that. This conception, which has many parallels in the dominant conception of Islam (as 'submission' to Allah), can be traced back to the early church Fathers. So Evagrius of Pontus described the theologian as 'the man who prays', and even the rational St

Thomas Aquinas (*c.* 1225–74), towards the end of his life, had what he regarded as a divine vision in the course of which he realized that 'all I have written seems to me like so much straw'.[2] In other words, the divine vision, despite his previous attempts to define or at least describe it as carefully as possible by using human analogies, is finally glimpsed as ineffable, and the best response becomes one of silence.

Today, it is the silence not of humanity but of God that has become the central problem for both theology and liturgy. In *Racing Demon*, the play opens with an agonized prayer by the main character, the Reverend Lionel Espy, the team rector who is trying to bring some sense of meaning to his calling in an inner-city parish:

> God. Where are you? I wish you would talk to me. God. It isn't just me. There's a general feeling. This is what people are saying in the parish. They want to know where you are. The joke wears thin. You must see that. You never say anything. All right, people expect that, it's understood. But people also think, I didn't realise when he said *nothing*, he really did mean absolutely nothing at all. You see, I tell you, it's this perpetual absence—yes?—this not being here—it's that—I mean, let's be honest—it's beginning to get some of us down. You know? Is that unreasonable? There are an awful lot of people in a very bad way. And they need something beside silence. God. Do you understand?[3]

If we accept the central thrust of the non-realist argument— that God should be conceived as nothing more or less than the human creation and articulation of the area of our deepest concern, the religious requirement—then we have to understand that the words of our liturgies and the practice of our rituals is our attempt to gather together with our chosen community of spiritual 'soul-friends'[4] and give expression together in symbolic form to our deepest spiritual yearnings and our human longing for some understanding of 'the vast expanse of interstellar space, galaxies, suns, the planets in their courses, and this fragile earth, our island home'.[5]

To understand as fully as we can what we are attempting in our worship, even if it borders on the ineffable, is an exercise we need to perform, and is part of our responsibility if we are worshipping citizens in the pluralist world of belief and worship at the end of the twentieth century.

In most cases, our common worship will still be in the form of realist language, and we shall need to make a shift in our interpretation of the texts used if we are to worship with self-understanding and self-esteem. There are other options. These would include the path into less credal and more silent types of worship such as that practised for the last three hundred years or so by the Society of Friends. Or there can be what the American theologian John S. Dunne has termed a 'passing over' into the liturgies of other world faith traditions to come back to one's own energized and newly empowered by the diversity of worship forms.[6] But for the majority these options are less practicable. The fact remains that the majority of non-realists, after they have come to the point of abandoning their traditional beliefs, still maintain their attendance at churches of mainstream denominations and therefore continue to use their realist liturgies. That this is the case is clearly revealed in opinion polls taken on both sides of the Atlantic enquiring into contemporary beliefs of ordinary citizens. For example, a poll in *Der Spiegel* dated 15 June 1992:[7]

	1967 %	1992 %
Do you believe God exists?	68	56
Do you believe that humankind descended from Adam and Eve?	49	32
Do you believe Jesus was born of a virgin?	36	22
Do you believe that Jesus was raised from the dead?	53	42
Do you believe Jesus was God's son?	42	29
Do you believe in the existence of Hell?	34	24

If it is the case, as evidence such as this leads us to believe, that most traditional Christian denominations include significant numbers of non-realists among their congregations, then the language of worship and belief ought to be adapted to reflect this representation. But it will be no easy task. In an article entitled 'Freeing the Christian Church from supernatural fetters', Hugh Dawes argues that 'the shift in the fourth century from the language of a Jewish sect into that of the Greek world was no less great than what is called for now'.[8]

It is clear from recent analogous discussions within traditional denominations that an attempt to redefine doctrines in a liberalizing or radical direction will meet a fierce rearguard action from traditionalists, Indeed, the possibility of denominational schisms between liberals and traditionalists has come to the fore of the agenda of many churches in recent years. As an example, we can observe what has become known as 'The Controversy' within the Southern Baptist Convention in the USA from 1979 until today. The Southern Baptists are a powerful traditional denomination in the United States commanding a membership of 14 million, comprising some 37,700 churches and six seminaries. Although in principle each congregation is self-governing, during this century the denominational machine working under the aegis of the Southern Baptist Convention (SBC) managed to impose a remarkable degree of uniformity on the theology and liturgy of the participating congregations. But since the 1970s this uniformity has been threatened by the insurgency of conservatives who held to the doctrine of 'biblical inerrancy'. This is the belief that the Bible is without error in all matters of faith, history, theology, biology, or any other issue that can be discussed in its light.[9] By manipulation of SBC elections from the Summit at Houston, Texas, in 1979, and the election of Adrian Rogers as president, the conservatives took control not only of the Convention with 'inerrancy' as their shibboleth, but also over publicity and educational materials, and influenced faculty appointments in the seminaries that are all voluntarily funded through the Convention. The moderates attempted to maintain a voice through the vice-presidency, electing Abner McCall (president of Baylor University) as Rogers's vice-president, but they gained little substantial power-base in the Convention, and in May 1991 6,000 disaffected SBC members met in Atlanta to form a new Cooperative Baptist Fellowship and to sponsor their own seminary.[10] Rather than stressing the conservative doctrine of inerrancy, the Atlanta Convention (which established the ongoing Southern Baptist Alliance) stressed the doctrines of 'the priesthood of all believers' and 'soul-competency', both of which traditional Baptist teachings stressed the right and ability of individual believers to interpret the Bible according to their own consciences and allowed for the toleration of a range of beliefs between the faithful. On the practical agenda of the more liberal grouping were placed the ordination of women (long opposed by the SBC on St Paul's grounds of the necessary subordination of women to men) and co-operation on projects with other denominations (ecumenism was not on the SBC agenda during the decade of the Controversy).

In fact, one of the developing features of our times highlighted by the example of the problems of the Southern Baptists is the lack of loyalty to particular denominations. In their weighty analysis of contemporary American religion, the sociologists Wade Clark Roof and William McKinney point out that 'switching' has become common: 'Less and less bound to an inherited faith, an individual is in a position of shopping around in a consumer market of religious alternatives and can pick and choose among aspects of belief and tradition.' They suggest that 'what matters is less the shared experiences and affirmations of a community of like-minded believers and more of a person's own spiritual journey and quest in search of an acceptable and fulfilling belief system'.[11]

It would be interesting to know how far this analysis would be appropriate to the situation in Europe and elsewhere. In our own country, there would presumably be different analyses of the rural, suburban and urban patterns. But a number of indications would suggest similar 'market forces' have come to be significant here—in each of these areas. Within the country, a very large number of Free Churches have amalgamated and a smaller number of Methodist congregations have developed ecumenical projects of co-operation with their neighbouring Church of England. In suburban areas, purpose-built estates of houses put up over the past 30 or 40 years include many ecumenical church buildings which have been built to be used by the major Protestant denominations, and are often combined with some sort of community centre. And in inner-city areas, certainly as far as the Established church is concerned, there scarcely exists any longer the concept of a parish church serving the local community. Nearly every Anglican church draws its congregation eclectically from a considerable area. Individuals and families seem to exercise their choice along the lines of churchmanship, degrees of conservative/liberal theology, and perhaps still a key factor is the particular personality of the minister-in-charge.

With denominational loyalty significantly loosened, there is another factor which might indicate that the other mainstream denominations will follow the course of the Southern Baptists and split into conservative and liberal factions. This is the combination of the democratic synodical structure of most Protestant churches, put in place and streamlined in the mass media age, and the complex moral issues of our times which have featured high on the synodical agendas. Thus, within the Methodist, Congregationalist, other Baptist, Presbyterian, Lutheran and Episcopalian denominations over the past ten to twenty years there have been numerous debates on the thorny subjects of extra-marital sex, abortion, divorce, homosexuality and AIDS (among others) which have resulted in split votes and divided synods. It has often been the case that the delegates of the Boards of these churches have divided almost down the middle on these subjects, creating thereby an even greater sense of unease and sensitivity than if the vote had been heavily on one particular side.

Alternatively, the authoritative bodies have alternated between traditional and more radical statements, thus revealing clearly their own doubts on the subjects being debated. For example, the Church of England in 1979 received a liberal report on homosexuality pioneered by Bishop John Yates, then Bishop of Gloucester. In 1987 this was followed by the Osborne Report, equally liberal but this time unpublished (despite the objection of Yates among other bishops) because of possible adverse reaction. In 1988 a debate in General Synod (including the House of Bishops) passed a motion which described homosexual relationships as 'falling short of the ideal' and homosexual practice appeared to be outlawed. Then in 1991 the House of Bishops produced a statement, *Issues in Human Sexuality*, which appeared to condone adult lay homosexual relationships whilst outlawing them among the clergy.[12] This most recent report attempts to preserve the Anglican 'principle of unity' by conceding major ground to both evangelicals (through its significant scriptural component) and liberals (through its basic acceptance of the non-judgemental premises of modern psychology). But one is left with the impression that the compromise is so patent as to carry weight with neither side in the debate at the end of the day. Basic conclusions seem to be irreconcilable here. Just as, in the Southern Baptist debate, the 'inerrants' could not conceive the real possibility of human error in the text of the Bible, so here conservative churchmen would fail to allow any account of human sexuality to be sufficiently evangelical and convincing if it condoned any form of sexual practice outside heterosexual marriage. And so we face a real impasse. On this and other issues, despite the publication of reports implying the existence of an authoritative consensus within the denomination, the actual situation contains a pluralism of attitudes, some based substantially on the Bible with a reference to modern society, others based substantially on contemporary experience with a biblical quotation or two. Many of the attitudes adopted in the consideration of these issues would appear to be mutually contradictory, so that presently any denomination can contain a complete range of ideas on the issue in question.

We must doubt whether the present position is tolerable for very much longer. If denominations remain deadlocked in their common policy on so many vital issues of our time, then how is real community growth to be achieved within those denominations? Will not the impasse of disagreement lead inevitably to spiritual frustration and ecclesial sterility? A possible solution to this dilemma remains a realignment of Christians not along the lines of outmoded denominational loyalties but rather along the lines of the different divisions on the theological spectrum. A conservative–liberal split such as that which has occurred among the Southern Baptists in America would be one model for denominations, but other realignments are possible. For example, a three-way split between conservatives, liberals and radicals might allow non-conservatives to opt for a realist or a non-realist revision of theology, and this might more accurately reflect present divisions of emphasis in some denominations. It may also fit more naturally into the lives of some. The Church of England, for instance, has for the past century or so been divided into three distinctive churchmanship categories: Anglo-Catholic, Broad and Evangelical. But with the almost complete success of the liturgical reform and the parish communion movement, it may be questioned whether these divisions are sharp enough to perpetuate. Do other divisions not rankle more?

Whatever the future will hold, for the present those who hold a non-realist understanding of faith remain largely in mainstream denominations, in communion with many believers for whom realism is the essence of faith, and participating in liturgies whose form and content reflect a realist understanding of God and the world. How does this situation affect us non-realists? According to Don Cupitt, it leaves us with a paradox: 'It seems that we must belong to the church and that nevertheless we cannot belong to the church.'[13] He goes on to argue that as radicals find themselves as part of established churches, even though at odds with them on many counts, we should stay and fight our corner by three tactics which he terms 'evasion', 'deception' and 'organized dissent'. These he regards as essential paths both for the integrity of non-realists and for the sake of correcting the reactionary movement of the church as an institution, which he believes is 'ghettoizing' itself and reasserting a Platonic dualism as the very requirement for membership in its 'subculture'.

Without wishing to dissent from Cupitt's analysis, in this chapter I wish to examine some of the liturgies at present in use, and consider how a non-realist understanding and use of their language would work. This is not to argue that *all* realist liturgy can be understood in this way, or that *any* form of worship is useful. Indeed, I would want to agree with the Reverend Lionel Espy in *Racing Demon*:

> So much of what passes for religion is simply nonsense.
> Close the church doors and all tell God how wonderful
> he is. 'God, you're so terrific. No, really. Terrific.' Where
> does that get you? And the more people doing it, the more
> you're said to be thriving. It's phony. It's spiritual
> masturbation, that's all.[14]

Since most worship, at least that worthy of the name, consists of rather more than the blind submission to God of this variety, there is a lot more potential for evaluation and human understanding of what is going on within the words and forms of the particular community tradition of which we are part and whose language we share.

The juxtaposition of words, music and images provides us with a dynamic which we can use creatively to build up our human understanding and our capacity for the good. But to use this material creatively we have to be sensitive to its nature. A lot of it we have inherited, and as an inheritance it is part of a culture not our own, part of that great stream of history, the past, of which L. P. Hartley speaks so poignantly at the beginning of his novel *The Go-Between*: 'The past is a foreign country: they do things differently there.'[15]

So we have to be knowledgeable about the developing history of the tradition we have chosen to work within, and realize that it has developed a highly sophisticated language system to connect its adherents to the source of its perceived spiritual power. So, in a fascinating analysis of the role of creeds in postmodern society, the American George A. Lindbeck describes how to become a Christian 'involves learning the story of Israel and of Jesus well enough to interpret and experience oneself and one's world in its terms'.[16] In Lindbeck's understanding, doctrines do not therefore *make* but *regulate* truth-claims. They are a way (and only one way) of giving us a chosen handle on the world we inhabit. Lindbeck is quite content to treat them as nothing other than useful tools for our understanding. He does not deem it necessary to enquire any further into their meaning: 'If doctrines such as that of Nicaea can be enduringly normative as rules, there is no reason to proceed further and insist on an ontological reference.'[17]

In other words, we do not need to be convinced of the actual truth of the statements of faith, such as the Creeds, to participate in their liturgical usage. We can use them as maps which provide us with convenient reference-points in our attempts to locate religious reality. Rather than viewing credal formulations (or for that matter biblical passages) as anchors, perhaps we should use them as buoys to chart our progress. And a number of navigational systems may help us to chart where we have gone and where we may be sailing. Richard Rorty has used this metaphor of sailing to describe post-moderns as 'Emersonian sailors, self-regretting creatures, adrift on Neurath's boat —

forever inventing and creating new self-images, vocabularies, techniques and instruments in light of the aweful backdrop of mortal beliefs and values which have no philosophic foundation or transhistorical justification'.[18] We should recall that within our liturgies the Creeds are dramatically recited and thus embody communal recitations of past history. Stephen Mitchell has spoken of how in leading recitation of the Creed in the Anglican liturgy, he likes to compare the exercise to reciting epic poetry.[19]

Here as elsewhere, much of a non-realist appreciation of liturgy will require a certain use of the imagination, what Samuel Taylor Coleridge termed 'the willing suspension of disbelief'.[20] In his own works, the advantage of this 'alteration in key' from the world of fact to fiction is best illustrated in his epic poem *The Ancient Mariner*. In this poem we observe how religious language becomes an extension of the poetic; the work concerns the centrality of prayer and the relationship between the self and the world of Nature, both inextricably linked for the writer:

> He prayeth well, who loveth well
> Both man and bird and beast.[21]

In blessing the water-snakes at the height of the poem, the Mariner blesses not just the representatives of all life, but is acknowledging and blessing in himself things which had previously disgusted and repelled him. So the spiritual 'nine fathoms deep' may be interpreted as the region of spiritual power from which the springs of salvation are released after he has performed the blessing:

> The self-same moment I could pray;
> And from my neck so free
> The Albatross fell off, and sank
> Like lead into the sea.[22]

Here is an account of alienation and reconciliation, between the self and the world, and the self and the Self. Prayer is experienced as freedom from the bondage imposed by the alienating forces and as a liberating experience making connections between the human world and the natural world of which humankind is one contributing part. In the religious vision, the barrier dividing Nature as subject and object is lifted in the imagination and a universal harmony is re-established.

What Coleridge's poem here imparts to us in vivid and romantic form is, I would suggest, the same type of dynamic which occurs through the sacramental liturgy of the church. Of course, the assumption behind this assertion is that, in the words of Gabriel Marcel, 'the more deeply one penetrates into human nature, the more one finds oneself situated on the axes of the great truths of Christianity'.[23] But this is precisely how a non-realist reads the richest resources provided by the Christian tradition. By attempting to describe the great powers 'out there', it has sounded the depths and revealed the outlines at least of the fundaments of our own human existence.

This has been most freely admitted within traditional liturgies in the branch of sacramental theology. The common understanding of a sacrament is 'an outward and visible sign of an inward and spiritual grace'. In this definition we do not, for once, have direct referencing to 'the things above', and we have an indication that interpretation is the key to sacramental understanding. The signs point to a meaning other than the literal, and the key of interpretation (*crux interpres*) is therefore to look in the direction in which they are pointing. In the Eucharist, for example, from the time of St Paul onwards participants were warned not to approach the sacrament carelessly, but to 'discern the body' in the action and so partake of the full benefits the sacrament offered.[24]

A non-realist can in a similar way stress the importance of 'discerning the signifiers' before the sacramental action commences. So, for example, Ronald Pearse (to whom Cupitt dedi-

cated *Radicals and the Future of the Church*) has produced an
'Explanatory Preface' which can be cited by the minister before
he or she begins the celebration of the Eucharist and which
indicates that the terrain about to be traversed can be understood in non-realist terms:

> A responsible spirituality is important for our health and
> for the well-being of the world. It can be supported by
> following a way of life within a fellowship. The Christian
> church is a fellowship which maintains and renews itself
> in the Eucharist, for which we have assembled. In this, we
> honour our historic myths and practice, discerning and
> using with integrity the content of our tradition and the
> opportunity of new insight, orienting ourselves anew in
> honesty, love and creativity.

Such a Preface could clearly be inserted before the rubric of
any chosen eucharist form.

Let us now look at the Order for Holy Communion, as
established by the Church of England, and see how the signs
may be pointing for a non-realist participation. This is a riskily
subjective exercise and is not meant to suggest *the* non-realist
meaning because, of course, this would be a contradiction in
terms. It is simply suggestive of the sense which the realist
language can make to participants of another cast of mind.
The service begins with The Preparation in which, after the
Introductory Sentences, the people confess their imperfections
and the minister proclaims their absolution. Here the signifier
points to the fact of brokenness — in common life the failure to
reach ideals set, the lack of authentic existence. By the admis-
sion of fault and the resolution to 'try again', the participants
undergo a spiritual cleansing whereby they become freed of the
dead weight of the past, what would hold them back from their
true future potential, and experience the liberation of being
freed from the thought of human imperfection. The authoritat-

ive pronouncement of forgiveness, reserved for the priest alone as 'ritual spokesperson', is a necessary sign of the certainty with which the future can be embraced. The power of the overcoming of estrangement has to be proclaimed clearly to be appropriated by the individual heart. Following the pronouncement of absolution the congregation experiences a feeling of renewal of the self, and a oneness with the source of individuality. One is genuinely at peace with oneself and there is also a solidarity with the others with whom one is worshipping, who likewise have experienced the grace of liberation from their former selves.

The Ministry of the Word follows, during which the congregation are invited to listen to the sacred history of Israel and the story of the Christ. Whether there are two or three readings from the Bible, the effect remains that we hear a number of sacred stories and we come to realize that none of the stories remains entire in itself: they act as pieces of glass in a mosaic to make up a composite picture. Only in the myriads and myriads of pieces do we see anything resembling 'a whole' and there is no whole apart from the building up of the fragmentary pieces, no biblical view, only collections of perspectives from the books that make up the Scriptures. The Ministry of the Word moves on to the Sermon in which the preacher adds his or her own stories to those already proclaimed, another mosaic through which he or she hopes further light will be refracted to the hearers. And then the congregation rises to proclaim together the regulation of fourth-century faith in the Nicene Creed. Here it seems to be important that the proclamation is communal. In traditional practice the sign of solidarity with fellow-worshippers is marked by the direction to turn eastwards to the High Altar. That this solidarity of expression may be a more important signifier than the precise content of the words recited is evident here as elsewhere in the sacrament, by the preference for Latin over the vulgar tongue, especially in 'high' celebrations and in the classical musical settings of the Mass.

The majority of those participating in Latin Masses have presumably never understood the individual words and sentences, but this understanding is less important than the sense of participation in a common proclamation of faith. The liturgical revisers underlined this perception when they altered the form of the Creed's introduction from the traditional 'I believe . . .' to the modern 'We believe . . .', so unveiling the truth that it was never meant to be read as a *personal* credal statement, but always as a statement of common purpose.

The Intercessions follow the Ministry of the Word. An extensive understanding of prayer from a non-realist perspective has been written by the contemporary Welsh theologian D. Z. Phillips.[25] A synopsis of this form of understanding is provided by Don Cupitt when he asks us to consider this sequence:

> I hope my friend Peter is happy; I think of him every day;
> I do it at a certain time of day; I say to nobody in
> particular, 'Let him be happy'; I say, 'O God, make Peter
> happy.' Why take this last step? The advantage of doing
> so is that I give formality, weight and seriousness of
> purpose to my care for Peter by binding it up with the
> moral and religious values that are most precious to me.[26]

If prayer is thereby an intensified concentration of the mind upon the other's well-being, communal prayer is also thereby a sharing of the concerns of the particular community gathered. For example, within the parish communion a list is often read out of the names of the ill and/or the deceased so that they can be commended to God's care. For a non-realist, this signifies the sharing of the concern with those gathered, a reminder of common mortality, and perhaps an opportunity given to show some practical concern later during the week for those in a position of need. In the American Episcopal rite at this juncture (which includes a choice of six forms of intercession as opposed to three in the Alternative Service Book), a concluding Collect stresses that the common binding of the concerns is a priority in the action:

> Almighty God, by your Holy Spirit you have made us one
> with your saints in heaven and on earth; Grant that in
> our earthly pilgrimage we may always be supported by this
> fellowship of love and prayer, and know ourselves to be
> surrounded by their witness to your power and mercy.[27]

The Intercessions are commonly followed by the exchange of The Peace, again a symbolic exchange amongst the gathered congregation expressing a unity of fellowship and purpose. In a gesture stipulated by the liturgical revisers but running counter to the taciturnness of English manners, the shared shaking of hands and exchange of hugs reminds even the most reluctant of participants of the spiritual links that have been forged through the worship between individual participants. This action also provides the opportunity to bury former animosities and relax relational tensions, as well as the chance to greet those also who would not be among the number of one's inmost circle. Thus the point is signified that Christian love is not in essence a mutual self-esteem, a backslapping of friends who can assist one another, but is a continual stretching out from one's family and friends (with whom one is presumably sitting) to embrace the neighbour and the stranger as the others whom we are bidden to love as well as ourselves.[28]

At this stage we reach The Preparation of the Gifts when ordinary representatives of the gathered community present very simple substances of food and drink, the bread and the wine, upon the altar. This is also generally the time when any financial collection is brought forward, all three offerings signifying the giving of the self in the service of others, a transformation not only of our understanding of what we have to offer, but also of our understanding of ourselves as givers as well as receivers.

The climax of the sacrament is the Eucharistic Prayer itself, the great offering begun by a dialogue between minister and people (the *Sursum Corda*) in the course of which the people give their permission to the minister to speak and act on their behalf. The speech and the action are together the transforming words and deeds which not only bring to the common mind a memorial of a sacred giving in the past (that of Jesus himself, through his suffering and death) but also recapitulate for those gathered the benefits in which that giving allows others to participate. In the eucharistic text the sacred words and actions 'take responsibility' for the offerings and in so doing they become a creative act which produces, for the believers, the life of Jesus himself for their food and their drink. The Breaking of the Bread suggests acceptance even in the fragmentation of our individual and corporate lives. There is ever wounding and being-bound-up in the process of crucifixion/resurrection.

The moment of reception of The Communion is commonly regarded as the spiritual zenith of the whole sacrament. The position is subordinate (often kneeling and/or previously making the sign of the cross) and the attitude passive (individual believers being fed, often orally, in what is a childlike attitude before the powerful feeding parent-figure). But the action is taken voluntarily by the communicants (there is always the permission to abstain) and this choice preserves the creativity of the individual communicants. All have taken upon themselves a fresh identity as 'little Christs' and directly fed by the divine now have within themselves the capacity to live out a god-like life in the week to come. Increasingly, mainstream churches have made this central element less exclusive than previously, since the offering of Christ's life is supposed to be an offering for all. Where previously the qualification for reception was Confirmation on the understanding that Communion entailed full church-membership, the trend is for the minister to announce that the table of the Lord is open to all, and for children as well as parents to come and partake freely of the offered food and drink.[29]

After the sharing of the bread and the wine, there remains little else of real significance to be performed. So the liturgical revisers have removed a number of sections (including the Gloria) that were previously situated post-Communion. The blessing and the dismissal locate the whole sacramental liturgy firmly in the context of service in the world. The final sentence is pronounced by the minister: 'Go in peace and serve the Lord.' This linkage is eloquently established in some words by Archbishop Oscar Romero:

> I have been learning a beautiful and harsh truth, that the Christian faith does not separate us from the world but immerses us in it; that the Church therefore is not a fortress set apart from the city, but a follower of Jesus who loved, worked, struggled and died in the midst of the city.[30]

The finale of the Eucharist goads the participants into action. As Stephen Mitchell put it, 'Faith is not a matter of truth, more of bearing fruit'.[31]

The sacrament of baptism has caused much controversy precisely because of the prevalence of a realist understanding of its signification. Much dispute continues in the traditional denominations over the age and degree of consent necesasry for candidates who wish to be baptized. While one denomination limits the qualification to those of adult years and the sign to full immersion, another claims that there is a 'baptism of the Holy Spirit' separate and distinct from water-baptism. Within the Established church, although children's baptism is the norm, there continues to be a variety of expectation as to the commitment and preparation required of parents and godparents/sponsors. The variation is from months of attendance and special classes to a single rehearsal for the service. Indeed, there are churches where even the latter is not a strict requirement!

Whereas a realist would require the debate to continue and be resolved on the basis of *the* most correct understanding of the sacrament, a non-realist would suggest that there is an infinite variety of understandings of the form of words and actions any one or combination of which may be appropriated by individual participants.

Within the service itself there are multiple indicators of meaning allowing the minister or the participants to draw out the particular emphases which they wish to underline. The Anglican service opens with a fairly wide-ranging elucidation of duties of parents and godparents, followed by the Ministry of the Word, within which a variety of biblical understandings of baptism are quoted. There is then the decision of the parents/godparents on their own behalf and/or (and this alternative is itself a moot point) on behalf of the candidate(s) for baptism. The mark of the cross is made on the forehead of the candidate (with or without 'holy' oil) and this is followed by the administration of the water. Even here, the rubric admits for a variety of practice: either a single or a threefold (= Trinitarian) administration, by either dipping or pouring. The ancient link between baptism of neophytes and the Paschal season is then reasserted by the donation of a lighted candle to the newly baptized, who are then welcomed into the fellowship of the particular or universal church (again dependent upon the stress given) with prayer.[32] There are many different interpretations of this liturgy. It has never been quite clear how far it ought to be a service in its own right (perhaps a private family celebration?) or how far it should be integrated into, say, a eucharistic setting. By admitting the pluriform nature of the sacrament and realizing that the combination of words and actions is flexible and permutable, we can use the set liturgy and adapt it to the kind of spiritual understanding we or our charges wish to make at an important juncture in their relationship with the church. As with the Eucharist, much of what occurs in baptism occurs in the perception of the participants and is not something that happens irrespective of these perceptions. For this reason, if for no other, non-realists would reject the traditional interpretation of sacraments as 'objective' signs of the action of God which occur for and on behalf of believers *whether or not* they subjectively realize the truth of their situation. Non-realists would hold that there is no objective sacramental truth existing independently of observation. Also, no bond which is established through sacramental action can be 'indissoluble' since all human meaning is infinitely adaptable and relative to the insights of the individual(s) involved in a particular nexus of signifiers.[33]

The two biblical sacraments we have examined, Holy Communion and Baptism, may have, I have argued, meanings which are appropriate to a non-realist and non-supernaturalist understanding of human life and reality. We can participate fully in their drama of sacred words and actions without any prior commitment to belief in an objective order or supernatural personality. Rather, the sacraments are like a particular type of spectacles which we need to put on from time to time to give us a clearer vision of how we fit into our community, to our society, and to our world, as participatory individuals. Just as we do not need to live and dress in Elizabethan costume to attend and learn from a Shakespearean play, so it is not necessary to have a realist mentality or to believe in a Father-God 'out there' to benefit from participation in sacramental liturgy. Especially where the set is grand, as in the British tradition of cathedral worship, involving the panoply of senses through the worlds of architecture, music, poetry, costume and dramatic presentation (nowadays much assisted by advances in modern technology), increasingly the individual attenders will not have particular commitments either to that particular diocese or to that specific form of belief. Indeed, Don Cupitt has suggested that cathedrals in contemporary Britain have now largely taken on the type of role played by Hindu temples in India, where a perpetual string of visitors/pilgrims queue for the administrations of the priests simply because they are on tour at that particular place at that particular time, to register (for themselves only) a 'presence' there rather than to make any particular commitment to that temple or indeed to the particular gods of that community. It is strange that many wish to deny the links between cathedral attendance and tourism (by objecting to charges, for example) or between cathedral support and commercialism (by objecting to sponsorship), when it is precisely the needs of pilgrims and the status of the city that led to the mediaeval erection of so many of these treasures of our national heritage. In other words, although the expressed aim of their building was *ad maiorem gloriam Dei*, the actual dynamic was one of a celebration of the diversity of local creative skills and a bringing together of artistic and technical knowledge to produce edifices speaking of the joy of human skill and creativity. If 'God' was cited as a focus for the creative activity, then in a realist world of hierarchies this was no bad thing, since his supreme glory was infinitely refracted in the lesser glories of his human creatures and his inanimate creations.

However, in the light of modern Western thought, non-realists will have great problems in continuing to maintain such a view. And this, not only because they regard the existence of such a Being as an illusory projection of human ideals, but also and perhaps more tellingly because the mediaeval understanding of the hierarchy of the universe is one that they would wish to reject, namely, one of relationships based in their essence on the principle of inequality of power. In that universe, animals were subject to humans, women to men, slaves to masters, laity to priests, monks to abbots, and men to angels in a way that was profoundly debasing of individuals within such relationships. Such an outmoded world-view produced a universal psychology of domination and submission which reached not only its final expression but also its ultimate justification in a realist theology, which placed God the Father at the top of the pyramid as the unquestioned and undefiable head of the whole order of

subjection and imprisonment within one's particular designated
role in the social nexus. As Cupitt has expressed it, 'the basic
fact of life, namely sexual domination, was hyped up, mythi-
cised, multiplied, made cosmic, controlled, yes, to some extent,
but also validated—by God the Father'.[34]

And a real problem of self-identity is here revealed. As the
quotation from *Racing Demon* above highlights so well, much of
traditional worship remains a paean to an almighty and jealous
deity who continually needs reminding by sycophantic
preachers and senseless choruses just how wonderful he (and
therefore the whole sado-masochistic order of creation he has
brought into existence and authorized and blessed) 'really' is.
Such fawning adulation can also wreak substantial damage on
the worshippers who fall victim to this psychological mindset.
A. N. Wilson astutely observes on this point:

> The believer is in pursuit of something much more
> palatable and attractive than the truth: it is the feeling of
> being loved 'Ransomed, healed, restored, forgiven, who like
> me His praise shall sing?' Religious egotism is the most
> potent form of egotism that exists. It can swell and grow
> and take over the earth. It begins with the simple egotism
> of believing that the Creator of Earth and Sky is perpetually
> engrossed in your personal moods, prayers, sins and
> virtues, and that He has gone to the trouble of inventing
> special punishments for you if you deviate from His law
> by thought, word or deed. The egotism flowers into the
> conviction that God was so worried about your sinfulness
> that He came down to earth in human form and died a
> painful and humiliating public death as a sacrifice for
> your transgressions. Anyone who is capable of believing
> these things has placed themselves, and their relationship
> with the Almighty, at the very centre of the universe.[35]

While maintaining as I have that the God-symbol can still

be maintained as a non-realist symbol, there are certain drastic alterations to its traditional understanding and usage in worship which must be effected if it is to remain a symbol which helps worshippers to be in touch with the hidden springs of their spirituality. The first and most obvious is that we need to challenge the continuation of the idea of a dominant patriarchal male supremacy of this type which enables the kind of regressive psychology criticized by Wilson to occur. This alteration can only be assisted by a more positive image of women than prevailing weakly projections of the Virgin Mary would allow.[36] Liturgical reforms are here lagging far behind theological insights. So even in the calendar of the Alternative Service Book, it has been pointed out that there are seven times more saintly men than women. And in the rare places where complementary male and female saints are given respect, an inability to perceive them on the basis of equality is revealed. For instance, while William Wilberforce makes his first appearance as 'Social Reformer, 1833', Josephine Butler appears as 'Social Reformer, Wife, Mother, 1906'. Clearly the underlying assumption here is that for women to achieve sanctity they need the extra qualification of continued fidelity to their traditional and subordinate family role.[37]

To release a spirituality less distorting and more holistic we need not only to re-establish the Eternal Feminine as a potent symbol of universal consciousness but we also need to restore the power of some other neglected elements of the hierarchical chain of being. These include elements of non-human life which are often more highly regarded in other religious traditions. Both Judaism and Hinduism have many more animals and images of animals in their structures than does Christianity. And, as so often, a return to the insights of the ancients here may help us to make the necessary adjustments. So the American theologian Mary Daly points out that the ancient Greek philosopher Paracelsus:

> Following sources from Greece, Egypt, India and China
> ... divided the elements into four groups: the gnomes
> (earth spirits), undines or nymphs (water spirits),
> salamanders (fire spirits), sylphs (air spirits). Elementals,
> thus understood, provide Radiant Words for Naming our
> spiritual connections with the elements.[38]

Liturgies therefore do need a broadening out, particularly along feminist lines, to release them from an outmoded hierarchism.[39] For the Church of England, a reworked non-sexist version of the Alternative Service Book remains a high priority for the year 2000.

As we progress towards the new century, the area of worship remains one of the greatest potential for non-realist development of the Christian tradition. Firstly, the worship of the Christian church has always been in a process of continuous development and revision. It has never been narrowly restricted (as have doctrinal developments) to the form of the biblical material, nor has an earlier stage ever been taken by any denomination as normative for all further developments of this tradition. Worship is not also, in its essence, primarily 'about' God (as it could be argued doctrine should be) but is an expression of devotion and evaluation by a particular community using the best and most appropriate means of expression available from its particular culture. Worship is also arguably a primary religious activity. The need to pray appears to precede the need for sophisticated explanations of how prayer is believed to function, and the worship of the church inevitably influences the way believers articulate their beliefs. This must be the indication of the patristic formula *lex orandi lex credendi*, the law of worship (becomes) the law of believing. By being inherently dynamic, necessarily different on every and each occasion, worship resists the close definitions that non-realists fear in the doctrinal arena and permits spontaneity and free expression in a form not permissible for a dogmatist.

The words of J. D. Crichton in his introduction to the comprehensive work *The Study of Liturgy* remain a challenge to non-realists who participate, with differing degrees of conscience, in the continuing worship of the churches of realist understandings and language:

> Liturgy does not lend itself to definition, but if one is to
> be attempted it could be stated as follows: it is the communal
> celebration by the Church which is Christ's body and in
> which he with the Holy Spirit is active, of the paschal
> mystery. Through this celebration, which is by nature
> sacramental, Christ, the high priest of the community,
> makes present and available to men and women of today
> the reality of his salvation.[40]

No given God, no unchangeable reality. We are worshipping neither a being out there nor yet ourselves. If we were to continue either of those courses, we would be victims of the 'cosmic egotism' exposed by A. N. Wilson and Don Cupitt, from which any religion worthy of its teaching must attempt to save its adherents. And so we worship, acknowledge a sense of worth, in those parts of ourselves and others that truly free us to creativity and a greater humanity. For a religion that called upon God to enter humanity and take on 'a human face' this is a natural progression, a sensible development.[41] If liturgies can give us a right sense of ourselves in our human context, and loving perceptions of the others with whom we are inextricably bound through our families and our society, then by our choice to attend them and to give them of our time and concentration, we can utilize them in service of a wider sense and value. For the church has always been most significantly viewed not as an end in itself but as an instrument of bringing the kingdom of heaven into the world. In our understanding, that means that our worship prepares us for lives of worthiness; liturgy is the text for full commitment to the panoply of human values, and gathering together in prayer is a way of saying with others: 'We want to be taken seriously. We want to take seriously. Let us give each other the chance not to exploit and injure but to work with and build up.'

The mystical vision remains the *summum bonum*. It includes, as in *The Ancient Mariner*, the tragic but necessary shedding of the albatross, but also the unity of self with the rest of the living world. Hurt is observed and acknowledged before we are free to move on to an appropriate obverse of that hurt, that is, the 'wellsprings of trust' and creativity that we can resource and empower in whatever directions we choose. The languages of liturgy can never, of course, give us a hold on that high vision. For the person who sees the face of God shall surely die. But it can offer to us a collection of interpretative tools which (if we are careful to select according to our highest human insights) can connect us with our deeper selves and with one another in a manner that frees rather than truncates our spiritual development. We are responsible adults in a random world who must exercise our choices carefully and with an eye on the people we wish to create ourselves and others to be. For if God is made in our image, we have the highest potential for human growth. Not the sky, but the depths of the human heart are our limit. Limitless.

Notes

1 Søren Kierkegaard, *Journals* (Indiana University Press, 1967), vol. 1, p. 11, para. 20.

2 Quoted by Frederick Copleston SJ in *Thomas Aquinas* (Search Press, 1976), p. 10.

3 David Hare, *Racing Demon* (Faber & Faber, 1990), p. 1.

4 A word derived from Kenneth Leech's book on contemporary spiritual devotion, *Soulfriend* (Sheldon Press, 1977).

5 Eucharistic Prayer C of the American Episcopal Rite, *The Book of Common Prayer* (Seabury Press, 1977), p. 370.

6 John S. Dunne, *The Way of All the Earth: An Encounter with Eastern Religions* (Sheldon Press, 1973).

7 Quoted by Don Cupitt in his paper *Non-Realism and God* at Sea of Faith V Conference (1992), p. 8.

8 Hugh Dawes, *The Times* (27 July 1992). Cf. also his *Freeing the Faith* (SPCK, 1992).

9 Bill Leonard, *God's Last and Only Hope: The Fragmentation of the Southern Baptist Convention* (W. B. Eerdmans, 1990), p. 7. Cf. Alan Neely (ed.), *Baptist Means Freedom* (Southern Baptist Alliance, 1988).

10 At the time of writing not yet housed in its own building but working out of Union Theological Seminary, Virginia. Cf. article entitled 'Southern Baptists: facing a deep rift', *New York Times* (15 May 1991).

11 Wade Clark Roof and Wiliam McKinney, *American Mainline Religion* (Rutgers University Press, 1987), p. 647.

12 Church Information Office, December 1991. Cf. a similar situation in the United Methodist Church of the USA where after four years' deliberation, a 23-member Commission reported that 'the present state of knowledge and insight in the biblical, theological, ethical, biological, psychological and sociological fields does not provide a satisfactory basis on which the church can responsibly maintain the condemnation of homosexual practice'. Nonetheless the same Commission found it necesary to publish a minority report to the effect that this modern consensus of knowledge 'does not provide a satisfactory basis upon which the church can responsibly alter its previously held position'.

13 Don Cupitt, *Radicals and the Future of the Church* (SCM, 1989), p. 100.

14 Hare, p. 64.

15 L. P. Hartley, *The Go-Between* (Penguin, 1958), p. 7.

16 George A. Lindbeck, *The Nature of Doctrine: Religion and Theology in a Post-Liberal Age* (Westminster Press, 1984), p. 34.

17 Ibid., p. 106.

18 Richard Rorty, *Philosophy and the Mirror of Nature* (Princeton University Press, 1979), p. 261.

19 Stephen Mitchell, in conversation with Joan Bakewell, *Heart of the Matter* (BBC1, 19 April 1992).

20 Quoted by Dennis Nineham in *The Use and Abuse of the Bible* (Macmillan, 1976).

21 Samuel Taylor Coleridge, 'The Rhyme of the Ancient Mariner' in William Wordsworth and Samuel Taylor Coleridge, *Lyrical Ballads* (Oxford University Press, 1978), lines 645–6, p. 31.

22 Ibid., lines 280–3, p. 17.

23 Quoted by Gerald Hanratty, 'The religious philosophy of Gabriel Marcel', *The Heythrop Journal* (October 1976).

24 1 Corinthians 11.29.

25 Dewi Z. Phillips, *The Concept of Prayer* (Routledge & Kegan Paul, 1965).

26 Don Cupitt, *Taking Leave of God* (SCM, 1980), p. 133.

27 American Episcopal Rite, *The Book of Common Prayer*, p. 395.

28 Leviticus 19.18; Mark 12.31.

29 Although the practice of children receiving Holy Communion was disapproved of in a statement by the bishops in 1991, the very fact that the statement had to be made reveals how the climate of understanding here is changing.

30 Quoted in Robert McAfee Brown, *Spirituality and Liberation: Overcoming the Fallacy* (Spier, 1988), p. 13.

31 Stephen Mitchell, quoted in *Loughborough Echo* (17 April 1992).

32 Cf. Thomas J. Talley, *The Origins of the Liturgical Year* (Pueblo Publishing, 1986), pp. 33–7.

33 The word used of baptism in the American Episcopal Rite, *The Book of Common Prayer*, p. 298.

34 Cupitt, *Radicals and the Future of the Church*, p. 114.

35 A. N. Wilson, *Against Religion* (Chatto & Windus, 1991), pp. 28f.

36 Cf. John Shelby Spong, *Born of a Virgin* (Harper & Row, 1992).

37 Cited by Ann Loades in a talk, 'The Virgin Mary and feminism', given at Southwark Cathedral (27 January 1990).

38 Mary Daly, *Pure Lust: Elemental Feminist Philosophy* (Women's Press, 1984), p. 7. The schema of the elements (*stoikheia*) was well established in a New Testament world-view; cf. Galatians 4.3–9; 2 Peter 3.12.

39 Cf. Janet Morley, *All Desires Known* (Movement for the Ordination of Women and Women in Theology, 1988).

40 Cheslyn Jones, Geoffrey Wainwright and Edward Yarnold (eds), *The Study of Liturgy* (SPCK, 1978), p. 28.

41 Cf. John Macquarrie, *The Humility of God* (SCM, 1978).

5 *Losing the Real for good*

Work out your own salvation with fear and trembling, for
it is God which worketh in you.[1]

If we create our own reality then we also create our own
meaning-systems and produce our own moral codes. In a way,
this is not so very surprising. All ethical codes and systems,
from the ancient Babylonian Code of Hammurabi to the French
Constitution, are the result of hard and careful moral thought;
all ethical systems betray in their wording the predominant
ideals and also the prejudices of the particular area within
which they have been formulated. They bear in them the signature of their authors and their language is inevitably a particular
cultural language. There is no universal written moral code.
Even the Ten Commandments, which were exclusively written
for the Jewish nation and to protect Jewish property rights, were
never adopted across national or racial boundaries. Indeed, the
very derivation of the word 'religion' signifies 'a bond' uniting
the individual with his or her particular moral code.

The nineteenth-century novelists recognized the close link
that obtained between theology and ethics, and were loath to
let go entirely of a system which had produced a reasonable
social equilibrium and seemed to provide citizens with a cohe-
sive meaning-system. It was Fyodor Dostoevsky (1821–81) who
first glimpsed the implication of the contemporary challenge to
religious belief when he saw that 'without God, everything was
permitted'. This was a terrifyingly stark conclusion to the
religious debate that had been sparked off by the Enlightenment

(*Aufklärung*) and in the science of the day was coming up against Darwinism. Some argue that it drove Nietzsche to madness and many others in our century to a religious despair. Equally, it was a conclusion to which many found themselves unable to grant their assent, not on the grounds of its logical truth, but simply because they found themselves terrified of the consequences of the doctrine for humankind if it were to be accepted as true. So the religious affairs correspondent of *The Times* spoke for many when he wrote:

> This contemporary faith in the vague universal benefit of any and all faiths renders the intellect incapable of making intelligent judgements. It is forced to say of Nazism, or ancient religions which practised human sacrifice, that they too are 'true' for their adherents, thus pulling the whole house of cards down.
>
> Mankind must remain capable of insisting, without qualification, that Nazism was false; and to see that religion has a dark side where terrible things can go on while still remaining 'true' to those who believe in them. It has to be able to say, furthermore, that what is wrong with them is not just their effects but their contents.[2]

Someone who realized just how evil Nazism was, and was prepared to give his life to remove the central perpetrator of it, was the Lutheran pastor Dietrich Bonhoeffer (1906–45). But Bonhoeffer was too honest to proclaim an absolute truth to support his case when he knew that none such existed. Realizing the extent of modern secularity, when he wrote from his prison cell that 'As in the scientific field, so in human affairs more generally, "God" is being pushed more and more out of life, losing more and more ground',[3] Bonhoeffer pulled no theological punches and hid behind no pious expressions. After his own direct involvement in the von Stauffenberg plot on Hitler's life and his subsequent interrogation by the Gestapo, in an essay

entitled *What Is Meant by 'Telling the Truth'?* he described how
much the truth of a word or situation is not in itself constant.
It is dependent upon the people being addressed; who is doing
the questioning and what is the subject of the discourse. He
cites as an example of the complexity of truth-telling the case
of the pupil who denied to his teacher that his father often came
home drunk. The bond between father and son is here a
stronger loyalty than the duty to tell an authority a piece of
gossip of little use to him in a school setting. What a responsible
decision entails here or anywhere is not the application of any
external yardstick to the situation but rather a sensitivity to the
precise details of the situation one is in. Ethical propositions
possess what he calls a 'specific gravity' which can be measured
only by the persons in the situation in which they find themselves: 'It is not only what is said that matters, but also the
man who says it.'[4] Thus no external judgement is able to be
made on whether or not Bonhoeffer was right to take part in
the plot violently to overthrow Hitler from power.

For Bonhoeffer, the good in a situation cannot be discovered
by *any* legal rule, is often paradoxical in nature, and is often
found in the area that transcends the human 'either/or' that is
apparent in any situation. Nonetheless, ethics remains primarily
a matter of choice, and, faithful to the Lutheran tradition, that
is seen as a matter for the exercise of individual freedom within
the particularities of the situation. It is noteworthy that few
modern theologians have written works on 'ethics', seeing it as
a branch (only) of systematic theology, while for Bonhoeffer the
work of ethics is crucially and in reality a practical activity and
one that cannot be avoided by the fine details of abstraction.
The basic task of the ethicist is to assist in the process of
choice. Bonhoeffer here quotes Goethe's Pylades when he says
to Iphigenia:

> Man's first and foremost duty is to go
> Forward and think about his future course:

For he can seldom know what he has done,
And what he now is doing even less. . . .[5]

Bonhoeffer witnessed in his life to the truth that ethical choice is not made in an academic vacuum but in the tussle of life and death, and his commitment in his own life-choices to Germany (rather than the United States) and the Confessing Church (rather than the State Church) brought his own life to an untimely end. And yet his witness remains firmly in his writings and in his fidelity to the truths of the Lutheran tradition he inherited in a time of world crisis.

Another contemporary writer for whom the secular experience clearly indicates the death of God is the Anglo-Irish novelist Iris Murdoch (b. 1919). Although she takes it as read that there is no independently existing objective personal deity, she shows concern both in her philosophical writings and in her novels for the consequent damage to spirituality that the demise of traditional religion has brought about in modern times. One of her novels particularly illustrates the connection between the death of traditional religious imagery and the loss of a convincing set of values.

In *Henry and Cato*, she examines the precise course of a loss of faith. In this novel, the developing lives of two childhood friends are described at the point when both are in their thirties. The one, a lecturer called Henry, returns to Britain from the States to claim a family inheritance. The other, Cato, is a priest. He has been working for about a year in a downtown Mission in Berkshire. After an agnostic youth, he had experienced a powerful conversion to the Christian faith and his single aim thenceforth had been the priesthood. Now, his lack of success at the Mission reflects his own growing doubts as to the claims of his faith. Over this year he has not articulated to any other person the profound change which was occurring within him, and yet he has felt it instinctively within him 'like a plant growing yet not able to be conscious of what the changes were which were daily taking place in its form and texture'. As a priest, this crisis of identity and belief became encapsulated for him in the deepest symbolic expression of Catholic Faith:

> He went on celebrating mass, each day, but the mass was dead to him, seemed literally dead, as if each morning he were handling some dead creature. He stood at the altar excluded, blind, unable to give any devotional expression to the anguish which he felt.[6]

In the very place where God's presence was commonly supposed to be total, where the priest himself assumed the role of Christ the divine one, Cato could only feel deadness; this emotion filled his soul with agony and threw him into a questioning despair. Unable to know whether he ought to 'stagger on' under the burden of this unbelief or not, he turns to his fellow priest Brendan, a Downside-trained Catholic, who genuinely tries to convince the doubter that he is experiencing the familiar trial of 'the dark night of the soul', that absence of meaning which the mystics have seen as a necessary part of their spiritual journey. Cato refuses to accept this traditional justification of his experience. For as an Aristotelian rather than a Tillichian, he accepts an either/or viewpoint on the question, and his darkness appears to him as unquestionably empty. The only alleviation he is offered for his crisis appears to him to come from a working-class boy to whom he finds himself attracted. Beautiful Joe, whom as a pastoral charge he had taken under his wing at the Mission, seems to wish to remain with him, at least. But this love he discovers to be as ambiguous as his loss of faith, and instead of comfort brings him only a disturbing vision for which no ready explanation seems to be available, either in pastoral manual or dictionary of psychology. Trying again to pray, as he had once been able to do, in the darkness of the night, Cato 'gazed into the darkness and the darkness was not dead but terribly alive, seething and boiling with life.

And in the midst of it all, he saw, smiling at him, the radiant face of Beautiful Joe.'[7] His dilemma now becomes total, since it is simultaneously reflected on the levels of his intellectual position, his professional status, and his emotional life.[8] These questions become so all-pervasive that he finds himself unable to quell their collective force in incapacitating him in his function as a priest. So when he goes to visit Joe's mother, he summons up his strength to act the role of the comforting minister, and yet the response he receives paradoxically reflects his own consciousness of the utter senselessness of hackneyed Christian formulae of salvation:

> 'Mrs Beckett, forgive me for speaking to you, but I am a
> priest and you are, whatever you say, a Catholic. . . . You
> must find your way back to hope and joy again. The way
> is open if you will only take it. The way is Christ, the
> hope is Christ. Take your burdens there and receive His
> love, hide yourself in His love and be healed. Don't
> despair. Whatever has happened, the world can be made
> new and good again. Come to church, why not, come to
> mass. I don't know what your troubles are and I didn't
> come here to question you or to pester you. But I wish
> so heartily and so humbly that I could help you. Come to
> church sometime, just sit there perhaps. The love of God
> is with you if you will just breathe quietly and let it fill
> you.' 'Fuck off,' said Mrs Beckett. . . .[9]

Although he has been able to recite these orthodox words with considerable aplomb, Cato realizes in this monologue that he is only using the patter he has been taught for his profession. The link between this language and the divine reality to which it purports to refer has for him, as apparently for Mrs Beckett also, become irreparably truncated. And yet this is the comfort he had genuinely tried to offer her in her spiritual distress. It was the sum of what his faith had to offer any soul in distress, the component claims of salvation which had to be accepted to lead to peace of the soul. And yet, if this vital link had actually been severed, 'if these words were false, then there was no consolation'. Neither for Mrs Beckett nor for Cato himself did the claims for the love of God seem to make any more sense. All they faced was a wretched confusion and a powerlessness, which in her case had found expression in the anaesthetic of drink. For Cato it was unalleviated. The future for him was not only unceratin but bleak in the extreme. Deprived of all his former certainties, his hope had deserted him completely. He could only face personal diminution and loss as the indisputable facts of the existing order. For himself, he could only find his identity henceforth in relation to these indisputable factors, and therefore the vitality of life as he had once known it in faith had been fatally transformed to a bare survival of self after the loss of real feeling and imagination.[10] Cato finally accepts his unbelief after his struggles and thereby embraces a new nihilism:

> While I was gazing at Joe in a dream it was all taken away, the high edifices of my faith were dismantled: the three-personed God, the Fall and the Redemption, the life of the world to come, *in saecula saeculorum*. Now there is only sin and woe and no saviour. Jesus was not the Son of God, he was just a victim, just a good witty man with a delusion. And so my life has become tiny and mean and incomplete and I must begin it again without comfort and without magic. It is the end of the story, and what follows will be quiet and dull, and I am fortunate that it is so and that I am not crippled and I will not even be miserable for ever.[11]

By force of circumstances, the outcome of Cato's spiritual journey becomes even more tragic than he had here envisioned. Through a bizarre collection of events (typically Murdochian

in their strangeness) in which he accidentally kills Joe, he comes
to the truly Nietzschean conclusion that with no religion there
are concomitantly no set bounds of morality, and he reaches an
equally Nietzschean state of subdued lunacy as he realizes and
appropriates the shocking consequences of his action. Outside
the bounds of the effectual compassion of any of his family or
friends, he exists in the realization of the actuality not only of
divine but also of human death. 'Death is the great destroyer
of all images and all stories', he muses, 'and ordinary human
beings will do anything rather than envision it.' Because he
has experienced in his life-crisis 'the non-existence of God as
something absolutely positive', Cato is now beyond the help
which any of his fellow mortals may offer him. They all so wish
to help, and yet their definitions of his reality and theirs fail to
plumb the depths of his experience of divine and human loss.

In the final scene, we witness the poignant leave-taking of
Cato and Brendan. Brendan, tired himself of the game of theological definitions, has decided to go out to Calcutta, to be
involved practically with the church's mission of healing among
the poor. Having realized that he cannot bring Cato back to
the faith, he finally admits to him his own belief that God is
not a person *simpliciter* but rather that transcendent Other that
makes of every definition the church may concoct an illusion
because of its far surpassing greatness. Joined thus in a common
agreement to depart on their separate new paths, Brendan
presents his friend Cato with the gift of his own crucifix, which
Cato willingly takes on his journey to Leeds, where he is going
to teach. We leave them thus as they depart in their respective
phases of faith and unbelief, joined however by the bonds of
suffering and death of which the cross of Christ will remain for
ever the compelling symbol. Though they are irreparably iso-
lated from now on by their separate goals, they are bound by
the spiritual principle of this cross. Asks Cato in leave-taking
of Brendan:

'Will you write to me?'
'I doubt it.'
'Will you pray for me?'
'Every day.'[12]

Here we may see that the experience of divine absence is known in contemporary culture not only by those like Cato who feel compelled to abandon their tradition, but also by those like Brendan who, while questioning, remain faithful to their Christian ideals. But the latter group ought not to be construed as having *more* faith, or some revelation of resurrection which the former have not been given. If they had, would they not attempt to share it more effectively with those for whom the tradition has become too remote for them to remain in harmony with? Those who wish to remain inside use the orthodox explanations of *El abismo de la fe* and the ineffability of God. These elements have always had significance for the mystics. They are today being incorporated into the very structure of the faith-system to account for our contemporary lack of conviction concerning any dogmas. Those who leave, however, have said that they will not be convinced by this manoeuvre, for in their eyes they have already tried this themselves and it has finally proved unhelpful in either locating their spiritual state or suggesting possible spiritual goals. No one can escape his or her own choice as to which of these alternatives he or she is to espouse. By remaining within the tradition and attempting to reapply its given symbols (through a God of liberation, or whatever) some may indeed claim the apparent support of an ever-developing institution. Others, by rejecting as untrue the claims of their tradition, witness to their honest search for truth that compels in an apparently meaningless world. Each of us today who comes from a religious tradition within the Christian West has to opt for:

A life of doubt diversified by faith,
Or one of faith diversified by doubt.[13]

So Murdoch's atheist position was fairly firmly established through plot-lines such as this. In many respects, she had reached an even more secular world-view than Dietrich Bonhoeffer. Thus she argued in her leading philosophical essay *The Sovereignty of Good* that 'there is, in my view, no God in the traditional sense of that term; and the traditional sense is perhaps the only sense. When Bonhoeffer says that God wants us to live as if there were no God I suspect he is misusing the words.'[14] And yet the attempt to discover religious meaning did not abate in her novels, and if anything their explicitly spiritual content grew throughout the 1980s, featuring a number of specifically religious characters for whom the truths of Christianity were still very much on the agenda.[15] And yet these characters do not by and large portray traditionalist Christian positions. By this stage of her writing, Murdoch had become aware of attempts to revise Christian doctrine along lines comparable with the contemporary scientific world-view. So, in 1978 she told a French audience:

> It is . . . interesting that after a period of irreligion or
> relative atheism there have been signs of a kind of
> perceptible religious renewal in certain changes in theology
> . . . in England one is experiencing a demythologization
> of theology which recognizes that many things normally or
> originally taken as dogmas must now be considered as
> myths. In this there is something that might have a
> profound impact on the future which, for the ordinary
> person, might return religion to the realm of the
> believable.[16]

What is necessary for this to be achieved is a complete overhaul of the modern concept of personality and thus human relationships. We have inherited, Murdoch argues, far too shallow an understanding of human meaning, and our philosophical tradition swings between two incomplete extremes: the Oxford linguistic tradition has become imprisoned in the logic of a grammar irrelevant to ordinary lives, while the dramatic language of choice adopted by Sartrean existentialists allows no scope for individual continuity of the personality or moral growth. Murdoch wants to break through these incomplete extremes to found a more convincing doctrine of the human self in relation:

> We live in a scientific and anti-metaphysical age in which dogmas, images, and precepts of religion have lost much of their power. We have not recovered from two world wars and the experience of Hitler. We are also heirs of the Enlightenment, Romanticism, and the Liberal Tradition. These are the elements of our dilemma: whose chief feature, in my view, is that we have been left with far too shallow and flimsy an idea of human personality.[17]

What Murdoch sees as necessary to a profound rediscovery of the human personality is a 'reorientation' of moral language, using the language of 'attention' and observation, which she has herself learned from the writings of Simone Weil. What obscures moral perception is the intricate web of deception, self-aggrandizing and the consoling dreams which prevent one from an accurate observation of one's own state in life or relationships. The individual psyche is in Murdoch's largely Freudian analysis a highly irrational collection of forces:

> An egocentric system of quasi-mechanical energy, largely determined by its own individual history, whose natural attachments are sexual, ambiguous, and hard for the subject to understand or control. Introspection reveals only the deep tissue of ambivalent motive, and fantasy is a stronger force than reason. Objectivity and unselfishness are not natural to human beings. . . . In the moral life the enemy is the *fat relentless ego*.[18]

Within a world of clashing egos and distorted perceptions of others, there remains that absurd place, 'the juxtaposition, almost an identification, of pointlessness and value'.[19] And it is by attentive and intuitive understanding of this space that we can learn to break through obscurity and come 'to see the place of necessity in human life, what must be endured, what makes and breaks ... so as to contemplate the real world (usually veiled by anxiety and fantasy) including what is terrible and absurd'.[20]

There is here and elsewhere in her writing a considerable amount of realist language and myth in Murdoch, and she seems to want to hold on to the Platonic myth of the idea of the Good as the searching light revelatory of all. However, the application of this device alongside her doctrine of the absurd still reveals a markedly postmodernist inhabited universe. Nothing much predictable happens in a place such as that. And yet, through a resolved attempt to see as clearly as possible the situation and nature of the relationships one finds oneself in, the effect can be made to purge and purify the 'fat, relentless ego'. What is necessary to make this effort is the human ideal of 'loving-kindness', a loving regard in the dark world for the other persons and things with whom one, often by accident rather than design, comes into contact. Trying to penetrate the superficial layers of human discourse to plummet the profound depths of mutual regard and esteem becomes a self-validating exercise which has no end other than the possibility of self-transcendence. This is a changed consciousness, often brought about by a catalyst in relationships which involves the participants in facing an extremity of love or death (the two boundaries of our solitary existence as human individuals). Since none of us is at the centre of the universe, it is a necessary part of our moral education to be 'decentred' or 'unselfed', and much of our ethical endeavour is our human attempt at a genuine purgation of the 'fat, relentless ego'. By reviewing the self in the light of the reforging it has undergone by the searing experi-

ences of otherness and consequent attentiveness to it, a new
and deeper layer of the self is laid bare and so produces a more
experienced and also a more authentic moral person. Through
the painful experiences offered by ever-present Eros (in the
wider Greek connotation that Murdoch attempts to recover for
our contemporary situation), we witness an analogy to the
ancient monastic practice of *ascesis*, an unselfing, a ritual of
purification, disciplined, painful, but ultimately a therapeutic
route for reconnection of the self with its dynamic of action.

Iris Murdoch is well aware of how central this process of
purification is within the corpus of her novels. At her own
request, when her portrait was painted to hang in the National
Gallery, she was portrayed by Tom Phillips seated serene in
front of the backcloth of a favourite picture of hers, *The Flaying
of Marsyas* by Titian. In this picture, the god Apollo torments
fellow musician Marsyas who has been strung up after losing a
musical competition between the two. The significance here is
the representation of reason and human culture (Apollo) as
triumphant over the musical and bacchanalian forces (represented by Marsyas). In the myth of the cruel destruction of a
rival musician, we see the Good not simplistically as hero-figure
but as a symbol of ambiguous but effective power. And Apollo
was himself, Murdoch reminds us, conceived as the god of art,
that branch of human understanding that helps us to 'unself'
the world to glimpse reality.

The title of Murdoch's fourth novel is significant for the
understanding of the rest:

> The bell is subject to the force of gravity. The swing that
> takes it down must also take it up. So we too must learn
> to understand the mechanism of our spiritual energy, and
> find out where, for us, are the hiding places of our
> strength.[21]

The old bells of the abbey convent are heard throughout the

novel by the inhabitants of the 'alternative' religious community who dwell just across the lake. The abbess is the only figure who is capable of bestriding the division between these two religious worlds. And so it is significant when she seems to be able to summarize to Michael Meade, of the alternative community, the failures of each to live up to its ideal in the continuous entrapment of individuals in unequal and unsustainable relationships with one another, in situations which seem to knock at their mettle so fiercely as to chisel new features into their moral fibre:

> Remember that all our failures are ultimately failures of love. Imperfect love must not be condemned and rejected, but made perfect. The way is always forward, never backward.[22]

It is curious that, despite the prevalence of love and its manifestations as a central component of the material of her novels, such a relationship even in its more refined forms is not in itself the means of *ascesis*. The characters in *The Bell* are paradigmatic of most of the characters in Murdoch's novels. They come and go in unusual and melodramatic encounters, and it is in these encounters, be they comic or tragic, that the readers glimpse the moral realities that seem to emerge from these interactions. The characters seem to discover in the course of the plot unfolding a truer self-knowledge through the mirror of the other. They emerge through their respective experiences rather as Jacob from Penuel, scathed but still able to walk, and aware of an encounter with something of great mystery and awe. What this is, is seldom articulated, although in the novels it is increasingly spoken of by use of the specifically 'religious' characters. The reader is left to sketch in the connecting links between the dots to make up the meaning of the 'full' picture of what the novel intends to convey. A 'good' is sensed but is not locatable in any one part or person of the action.

The personalities in her novels also seem rather boundless, with characteristics overflowing from one to another. They are also intensely introspective, but, in Murdoch's defence, the task of moral penetration has never been an easy one, and the complex interweaving of lives, feelings and occupations which constitute the fabric of human lives is not ever legible as an easy formula of description.

If the central problem in ethics is an obfuscation of issues and relationships through a myopia brought about by ego-centricism, then the way out of that maze needs a good deal of concentrated effort to counter the habitual laziness and cowardliness of the ethical self. The novels also reveal the importance of discovering a spiritual guide such as the abbess in *The Bell* and of maintaining a healthy maieutic relationship with that person. 'Unselfing' is an interior and ongoing process of spiritual attention requiring a more objective view of the self and its action than can reasonably be monitored by the self through its own perspective. The skill is to discover such an authoritative guide, without losing the sense of responsibility for one's own moral map and its contours. It can be achieved by a partnership, or a shared vision, but the problem is to try to avoid the pitfalls of an overbearing and dominant guidance so that one may have the necessary freedom of space within which we are each bound to make our own life-choices. I cannot allow any other person to shoulder that responsibility for my life since this rightly falls upon me. Anything less would fall back into the falsely objective way of living according to the expectation of others, which Sartre characterizes as *mauvaise foi*.

The difficulty with moral choice is that it is not an area where authoritative statements have much use or carry much weight. If the area of ethical concern is not a simple question of black and white but the mainstream of common living, namely the murky area of the grey, then clear and precise statements that the issue is black or white will be read as ill-informed and naïve, or wanting to produce a false certainty which would not come under the heading of 'faith' at all (but rather of 'knowledge'). Traditional religious systems do not wish to concede lack of understanding or competence in any particular area of knowledge. Therefore they prefer authoritative statements to silence or ambiguity. But those statements can very often reveal the lack of sure knowledge that their promulgation was intended to deny. Kierkegaard spotted this paradox in the founder of his particular Christian tradition:

> When one reads Luther one gets the impression, rightly enough, of a sure and certain mind, of one who speaks with a decision that is authoritative ('he preached with authority' Matthew 7.29). And yet it seems to me there is something disturbing about his certainty, which is in fact uncertainty. It is common knowledge that a particular state of mind often tries to conceal itself beneath its opposite. One encourages oneself with strong words, and the words become even stronger because one is hesitant. That is not deception, but a pious wish. One does not even wish to express the uncertainty of fear, one does not wish (or dare) even name it, and one forces out the very opposite mood in the hope that it will help.[23]

This is a very common trait in religious tradition as elsewhere, a variant of Queen Gertrude's 'The lady doth protest too much, methinks'.[24] There seems to be a natural abhorrence of a moral vacuum, and many people hold that it is better to fill it up with whatever words and explanations are available rather than leave it empty. Hence the current popularity of all types of fundamentalist doctrine and traditionalist morality. In 1992, the American presidential campaign took up the issue of abortion as a moral and political yardstick. The leaders of the Republican party seemed to believe that by vigorously espousing 'family values' (which were meant to include an absolute opposition to abortion under any circumstances) they would be a more electable party because of a clear rejection of any moral ambiguities (which had been personally admitted to in this area by both the President and the Vice-President of the party). This seems to be a case where the use made of the moral argument took on a greater significance than the content of the moral argument itself.

A non-realist approach to abortion, as to other ethical issues, would wish to remove it from such a political arena, and would also wish to re-emphasize that just as there is no absolute prohibition, so there is no automatic permission. There is no codified morality but only what Joseph Fletcher described some quarter of a century ago as a 'situation ethics':

> Gone is the old legalistic sense of guilt and of cheated
> ideals. When we tailor our ethical choices to fit the back
> of each occasion we are deliberately closing the gap
> between our overt professions and our covert practices.
> *This is an age of honesty.*[25]

In addition, the scientific advance of the West has placed us too readily in a rationalist frame of mind, in which we believe that a precise rational formula must be readily available in the region of moral choice as it is in other areas of our compartmentalized life. As Dietrich Bonhoeffer again clearly warned from the confines of his prison cell:

> We have spent too much time in thinking, supposing that
> if we weigh in advance the possibilities of any action, it
> will happen automatically. We have learnt, rather too late,
> that action comes, not from thought, but from a readiness
> for responsibility.[26]

When faced with moral choice, it is not only the rational but also the emotional and the volitional self which we call upon when we must make a choice. No matter how carefully the reasons for action are weighed, there remains the connection of the dots, the forming of the line of meaning, and this only can be effected by individuals as they plummet the depth of their spiritual resources and decide which pattern they wish to trace upon the world, which reality they will call up and pursue as their own. This can be a lonesome task but any attempt to evade it amounts to living a lie and should therefore be resisted in oneself and discouraged in others. The advice of the poet W. H. Auden is clear:

> The sense of danger must not disappear:
> The way is certainly both short and steep,
> However gradual it looks from here;
> Look if you like, but you will have to leap.[27]

In all the regulations which attempt to pattern our moral choices we have no more than human guidelines, sanctioned in the past by deities or reason, but nevertheless in our human view the position of a *particular* cultural time and place. The responsibility on our shoulders if we would wish to be adult ethical citizens is to exercise our moral autonomy in a way that respects our situation and the rights of those with whom we have to do. We cannot wait on the will of any external supernatural Being who (with whatever degree of neo-orthodox theological refinements) will decide for us, or predestine us on a particular course. Reassuring though such parental supports may feel, they remain a myth substantially denuded of real content by the state of modern knowledge.

The earlier stage of traditional religious belief was a very valuable preparation for our present period of ethical responsibility and should not be derided. On the other hand, to take what are now universally understood as cultural myths as truths determinative for our individual lives that we must take or leave as the price of our faith is a mode of bargaining we have to reject as illiberal and unnecessary.

We have in the Quakers and the Buddhists traditional groups of believers who sit loose to credal religion and moral codes but take their ethics no less seriously. The Sea of Faith Network among contemporary Christians in Britain is in the process of building up another such forum for those who wish to take one another seriously, as well as respecting the choice of each and all to create their own values and pursue their own vision of what goodness requires. As we attempt to take responsibility for our lives and times in this way, we can usefully be reminded of what Paul Tillich calls the demands of 'the Eternal Now'. We make our decisions aware that no identical choice has been previously made nor will one be made in the future. The uniqueness of the moment provides us with our opportunity. We should recall the words of George Fox: 'Christ said this; the apostles said that; what canst thou say?'

In our time, with the demise of realist theology and any denominational consensus, ethics has replaced mythology as the primary discipline and requirement for our enlightened response. We live in the age of the pragmatic rather than the theoretic, and by creating our own structures we produce a moral universe we can 'inhabit' and call our own, because we have brought it into being by our own language and our choice. Through the process of creativity as spiritual beings we can each of us respond in our own way to the felt human need 'to picture, in a non-metaphysical, non-totalitarian, non-religious sense, the transcendence of reality'.[28]

Notes

1 Philippians 2.12 (Authorized Version), quoted by Søren Kierkegaard as epigraph to *Fear and Trembling* (Princeton University Press, 1964).

2 Clifford Longley, 'Split between belief and ethics', *The Times* (29 December 1986).

3 Dietrich Bonhoeffer, *Letters and Papers from Prison* (enlarged edition; SCM, 1971), p. 326. Cf. 'God would have us know that we must live as men who manage our lives without him': ibid., p. 360.

4 Dietrich Bonhoeffer, *Ethics* (Fontana, 1959), p. 271.

5 Ibid., p. 246.

6 Iris Murdoch, *Henry and Cato* (Penguin, 1976), p. 49.

7 Ibid., p. 175.

8 One is reminded here of the close interweaving of motivations in reality for leaving the celibate state of priestly life. Charles Davis, the brilliant Catholic theologian of Vatican II, has expressed the thoughts of many on this interconnection in *A Question of Conscience* (Hodder & Stoughton, 1968). Also in *Body as Spirit* (Hodder & Stoughton, 1976), his post-Christian reflections on doctrine are dedicated 'to Florence, who first taught me the meaning of feeling'.

9 Murdoch, *Henry and Cato*, p. 196.

10 Cf. the experience which the poet Keats described as a 'posthumous life'.

11 Murdoch, *Henry and Cato*, p. 253, the conclusion of the first half of the novel, entitled 'Rites of Passage'.

12 Ibid., p. 399.

13 Robert Browning, 'Bishop Blougram's Apology' in *The Poetical Works of Robert Browning* (John Murray, 1929), vol. 1, p. 531.

14 Iris Murdoch, *The Sovereignty of Good* (Routledge & Kegan Paul, 1970), p. 79.

15 Cf. Charles Arrowby in *The Sea, The Sea* (1980), Sister Anne in *Nuns and Soldiers* (1980), Father Bernard in *The Philosopher's Pupil* (1983), and, perhaps most vivid of all, Father McAlister in *The Book and the Brotherhood* (1987) (all published by Chatto & Windus).

16 *Rencontres avec Iris Murdoch* (Université de Caen, 1978), pp. 16f.

17 Iris Murdoch, 'Against dryness: a polemical sketch' in Malcolm Bradbury (ed.), *The Novel Today* (Fontana, 1977), pp. 23–31.

18 Murdoch, *The Sovereignty of Good*, pp. 51f. (my emphasis).

19 Ibid., p. 87.

20 Iris Murdoch, *The Fire and the Sun: Why Plato Banished the Artists* (Oxford University Press, 1977), p. 80.

21 Iris Murdoch, *The Bell* (Penguin, 1958), p. 204.

22 Ibid., p. 235.

23 Søren Kierkegaard, *Journals*, trans. Alexander Dru (Indiana University Press, 1967), VI A 108.

24 William Shakespeare, *Hamlet*, Act III, Scene 2, l. 242.

25 Joseph Fletcher, *Situation Ethics* (SCM, 1967), p. 147.

26 Dietrich Bonhoeffer, *Letters and Papers from Prison*, op. cit., p. 298.

27 W. H. Auden, 'Leap Before You Look' in *Collected Poems*, ed. Edward Mendelson (revised edn; Faber & Faber, 1991), p. 313.

28 Murdoch, 'Against dryness', p. 19.

6 *Faith in the future*

The question facing the theologian today is, therefore, what can be salvaged from the eschatological wreckage?[1]

Hans Christian Andersen tells the tale of a youth who set out to learn what fear was. A father had two sons the eldest of whom was responsible and would clearly grasp success while the other sat at home with one wish—to learn how to shudder—which he could not understand. Hearing of his desire, the parish sexton arranged with the boy's father to take him back to his house where he had to toll the bell. It was to be tolled at midnight. Secretly the sexton stole in front of the youth and stood by the bell-rope as if he were a ghost. After challenging the stationary figure three times, the youth took a swipe at the figure, knocked him violently down the stairs, tolled the bell, and went home. On hearing of this outcome from the sexton's wife, the boy's father gave him fifty dollars and bade him leave his house. On route he had a bet of the fifty dollars with a traveller who believed he would learn to shudder if he spent the night at the gallows where seven people were hanging. Not realizing they were dead the youth took the bodies down and spent a contented night with them round the camp-fire. He was then guided by another sojourner to a land where there was a haunted castle where the king had promised his daughter to whoever could stay there for three nights. The king allowed the youth to take any three inanimate objects in with him, and he chose a fire, a turning lathe, and a carving bench with the knife attached. On the first night he met a cat with long claws with whom he swiftly dealt with his carving knife. Then he encountered hoards of black cats and dogs with fiery claws. But he dispensed with those in the same manner. Becoming tired, he espied a large bed in the corner but when he closed his eyes on it, it sped all round the castle until it crashed and threw him out. On the second night, half a man came down the chimney closely followed by another ugly half, and then more men arrived carrying skeleton legs and skulls. The youth rounded them on his lathe and then gambled with the skulls before he went to sleep. On the third night, six men arrived carrying a coffin, and inside the youth recognized his cousin who had died a few days ago. In trying to warm and revive the body, it rose up and attempted to strangle the youth who slammed it back in the coffin. Then a man with a white bear appeared and announced that the youth would surely know what it was to shudder since he was about to die. But the youth gained control of the old man's axe and anvil and was promised riches by the old man, but still did not learn what it was to shudder. The king rewarded the youth with marriage to his daughter, and though very happy at their union, he reduced her to despair because he still could not shudder. So the maid of the princess went out to the stream that flowed through the garden, brought in a pail full of little gudgeon, and at night the princess poured the pail of little fish over the youth so they swam all about him. And that night he learned how to shudder.

In attempting to 'explain' this curious tale, we should recall the warning of W. H. Auden: 'Dogmatic theological statements are to be comprehended neither as logical propositions nor as poetic utterances: they are to be taken rather as shaggy-dog stories: they have a point, but he who tries too hard to get it will miss it.'[2] Having reminded ourselves of the limitations of 'understanding' a story of this kind (and many of the parables in the Bible are stories of such a genre), we can at least deduce that one of the meanings of the tale is that the youth and his advisers were searching in the wrong areas of human life and experience to discover the key to anxiety. For this particular individual, a sexual awakening was necessary before any encounter with death would produce the desired reaction of fear. Only when the youth truly discovered what life was (with its deep erotic signification) would he be able to fear the spectre of death.

Just as this character in Hans Christian Andersen was pointed to, and looked in, the wrong direction for the discovery he longed to make, so it would appear many in our own generation, as previously in the Christian tradition, have been facing in the wrong direction to discover the meaning of faith for them.

For many, perhaps the majority, faith has been defined as a matter of logical assent to propositional truths that are located in an authoritative source (such as Bible, magisterium of the Church, or individual/charismatic person) and that is supposed to provide a superior connection to truth than anyone outside the community of the faithful could ever attempt to discover by any other means. So the 'pay-off' for membership of the particular Christian community is a collection of clear realistic propositions which are deemed to be held by every other member of that group. This is clearly a psychologically helpful device for group bonding. By reciting the words that the group have been uniquely offered, biblical, credal or liturgical, the individual members rehearse why they have left the company of 'the world' to come together with this particular collection of people. However, linguistically this may well rest on a mistake, since it appears to demand a particular epistemology or doctrine of reality, namely the 'correspondence theory' of truth with which many philosophers of language today would take issue.

There is another understanding of faith which runs counter to this, the differing logic of which has been carefully explored in the 1978 Wilde lectures of Natural Theology at Oxford by Professor Richard Swinburne.[3] This would be with the emphasis on faith not as a collection of beliefs but as the means by which an individual lives, generally taken as in relationship with God.

This is not under any understanding a variety of factual belief, it is *sui generis*,[4] an attitude to life which can be characterized as one of a basic trust and acceptance.

The contrast is brought out by the use of the definite article in the expression 'the faith once delivered to the saints', which suggests a theoretically definable collection of propositional statements, compared with the dynamic image of our faith as a spiritual quality which grows with careful nurture, such as in the parable, 'the kingdom of heaven is like a grain of mustard seed'.[5] One major distinction between these two definitions of faith is the question of history and science. A propositional understanding of faith must by definition be susceptible to historical and scientific criticisms. The propositions that constitute the faith are then either deemed to be immutable (in which case the real world is separate and immune from history and science) or have to be revised. And if the latter course is taken, then there remains the possibility that the content of the original proposition undergoes so much alteration by subsequent revisions that it becomes what the philosopher Anthony Flew has termed 'the death by a thousand qualifications'.[6] It has been argued that it is mistaken to attempt to see faith in this way from the point of view of New Testament criticism. As the leading New Testament scholar of our century put it back in 1924:

> But to what result has the course of historical criticism
> actually led? If it was at first directed by a confidence
> that such critical research would free men from the burden
> of dogmatics and lead to a comprehension of the real
> figure of Jesus on which faith could be based, this
> confidence soon proved to be delusion. Historical research
> can never lead to any result which could serve as a basis
> for faith, for *all its results have only relative validity*. How
> widely the pictures of Jesus presented by liberal theologians
> differ from one another! How uncertain is all knowledge

of 'the historical Jesus'! Is he really within the scope of our knowledge? Here research ends with a large question mark—and here it *ought* to end.[7]

And again:

But I often have the impression that my conservative New Testament colleagues feel very uncomfortable, for I see them perpetually engaged in salvage operations. I calmly let the fire burn, for I see that what is consumed is only the fanciful portraits of Life-of-Jesus theology, and that means nothing other than 'Christ after the flesh'.[8]

At the same time that Bultmann pointed out the difficulty of the model of propositional faith in an understanding of the Bible, the dogmatic theologian Adolf Harnack argued that the process of the Hellenization of Christianity had shifted the basic nature of the religion away from its evangelical origins into a totally rationalist system:

The assimilation of the Logos Christology into the faith of the Church . . . gave to the faith of the Christians definitely the direction towards the contemplation of ideas and dogmas, thus preparing the way, on the one hand, for the monastic life, and on the other, for a tutored Christianity of imperfect working laymen. It legitimised hundreds of questions of cosmology and of the nature of the world as religious questions, and it demanded a definite answer on pain of losing salvation. This led to a situation where instead of preaching faith, people preached faith in the faith and stunted religion while ostensibly enlarging it. But since it perfected the alliance with science, it shaped Christianity into a world-religion, and indeed a cosmopolitan religion, and prepared the way for the Act of Constantine.[9]

Rather than regarding faith as a firm foundation for propositional truth by which believers could be supported, and over the firm contours of which they could tread the path of revealed Christian truths, nineteenth-century radicals produced a metaphor of faith which owed more to that other tract of territory, the vast expanse of the sea. So Matthew Arnold laments the passing of religious belief in a poem he published in 1867 called 'Dover Beach':

> The Sea of Faith
> Was once, too, at the full, and round earth's shore
> Lay like the folds of a bright girdle furl'd;
> But now I only hear
> Its melancholy, long, withdrawing roar,
> Retreating, to the breath
> Of the night-wind, down the vast edges drear
> And naked shingles of the world.[10]

Although this image was developed with a concern for the diminishment of faith, it does have other connotations of use to the more dynamic concept of faith which we would wish to adopt in future constructions.

Whereas the land has fixed marks and plotable contours, the oceans are forever shifting. They have no agreed Archimedean point, and even the guiding buoys are floating. The vast expanse of interpretable reality is also more highlighted by the image of the sea, which stretches indefinitely and is amenable to the vessels we humans launch upon its expanse and the paths we chart across its waters. It is also deep, with our vision of it no more than a surface reality which conceals both animate and inanimate life beneath. Thus faith is for Søren Kierkegaard 'faith over 70,000 fathoms of water', that is, an attitude of mind and will, determined to plane the surface and not to be dragged down into the murky subconscious depths. This is one of Kierkegaard's most dynamic images but is developed from a curiously ambiguous Danish word *Tro* which has a cognate meaning, 'doubt'. In other words, 'faith' and 'doubt' are not mutually opposing forces but are in a paradoxical relationship. Doubt is possibly the 'shadow side' of faith that in its negative aspect, implying hesitation and fear, is banished by the free exercise of faith. So, 'the conclusion of belief is not so much a conclusion as a resolution, and it is for this reason that belief excludes doubt'.[11] Faith as an act of will is not universally defensible in terms of logic but as a way of describing the attitude which religious people adopt towards their cosmos is a viable description of a frame of mind which can create a meaningful framework out of a formless chaos. It was the philosopher Ludwig Wittgenstein who did most in our century to describe linguistic structures as constructions which produce an attempt to picture reality through a collection of word-games. Whereas Anglo-Saxon philosophers of language working with a more realistic critical framework had attempted to argue that all religious and ethical language was bad grammar and therefore senseless,[12] Wittgenstein allowed that religious language, as long as it followed the rules of its own grammar, was as valid a construction as 'scientific', 'historical', or any other human language:

> When someone who believes in God looks around him and asks, 'Where did everything come from?' he is NOT asking for a (causal) explanation, and the point of his question is that it is the expression of such a request. Thus, he is expressing an attitude toward all explanations. But how is this shown in his life? It is the attitude that takes a particular matter seriously, but then at a particular point doesn't take it seriously after all, and declares that something else is more serious. . . . Theology which insists on the use of certain words and phrases and bans others, makes nothing clearer.[13]

Wittgenstein here suggests that a universal understanding of theological language is an inaccurate assessment of how human language has developed and works. Within his understanding of language about God, a change of perspective is not only possible but necessary as we move from one type of description to another. Religious language includes within its rules of grammar the permission to alter our attitude (and therefore our perspective) as we pass from one form of linguistic description to another. But there is no central truth which can be perceived extralinguistically or which can illuminate and give a relative perspective on the various games we are required to play. The structuralists describe this as the loss of the transcendental signified[14] and without such a focus see human existence as a continued interplay of interlocking forces like 'a network of jewels in which each jewel reflects all the others and so on, to infinity, without there ever being a centre to grasp, a primary core of irradiation'.[15]

As soon as we have made the radical shift in vision which sees the universe we inhabit in this particular way, then our own faith and doubts are put in perspective. If we hold truth to be a matter of simple correspondence between a reality and its linguistic symbol, then faith becomes a trust in the connection and doubt a disbelief that they are thus connected. But as soon as we admit that our language is a multi-faceted and variable insight into the way things are, our faith and our doubt become more malleable. They become like different keys we use to modify our expressions, by our tone and by the degree of our commitment to the particular statement we wish to make.

Just as faith has had different emphases in the Christian tradition in the past, so too has doubt. Under the figure of the Apostle Thomas it has largely received a bad press. It is better, his story suggests, to pass beyond one's own hesitations about religious belief and to reach the point of real affirmation where one can exclaim 'My Lord and my God!', unimpeded by doubt.[16]

Doubts have a number of different flavours and are acceptable to the degree that the flavour is liked or disliked by the judging authorities in question. Historical doubts have already been mentioned, and can be castigated for detracting from the sacred wholeness of the text or the institution. In this area there are also doubts about destiny in history. So, for example, the American rabbi Richard Rubenstein in his monograph entitled *After Auschwitz* wrote that after the enormity of the concentration camps it was no longer possible for Jews or Christians to perceive God as the Lord of history.[17] Moreover, he suggests that this doubt springs from our moral sense and that it must pervade all future anthropology as much as theology. He quotes the psychoanalyst Erik Erikson: 'Our image of man must forever include the hell which was their last experience on earth.'[18]

Here the hesitation is in giving a meaning to a monstrous event in history that appears to defy all ordinary meanings. There can also be a more general hestitation about the giving of meanings as an existential process. Of this Jean-Paul Sartre (1905–80) says of himself 'Deceived and mystified to the marrow, I wrote with joy about the misfortunes of the human condition. In dogmatic fashion I doubted everything except that I was a soul chosen for doubt.'[19]

Doubters know and sympathize with such a self-view. Other doubters ply their doubt for what might be described as 'more positive' religious reasons, because the doubts show up the mystery and the fact that it can never be schematized by religious or philosophical systems of belief.

So the Spanish writer Miguel de Unamuno (1864–1936) had this in mind when he wrote:

> My religion is to seek truth in life and life in truth,
> conscious that I shall not find them while I live; my
> religion is to struggle tirelessly and incessantly with God
> as they say Jacob did from earliest dawn until nightfall.[20]

Such an exciting concept of doubt nevertheless remains

largely alien to gathered Christian congregations today who prefer, by and large, to perpetuate the dualist divisions which Realism is always in danger of inculcating. Most Christians are prepared to live in the secular world and adopt its values Monday to Friday and by 'the willing suspension of disbelief' are prepared to adopt a completely different world-view when they sit in their pews on Sunday. Although non-realists wish to encourage a pluralism of languages religious and secular, they want neither intellectual dishonesty of this variety nor a refusal to bring to churches the language and concerns of the commonly inhabited world. The present situation is one in which (in Cupitt's words) 'Somehow it is judged expedient to allow the know-nothings to define orthodoxy, and Christianity's once great intellectual tradition remains hidden in the decent obscurity of the academy'.[21]

Much of the blame for this sorry state of affairs inevitably is placed at the door of the clergy who, one would suppose, ought to provide the link between academy (in which most of them have trained) and pew. As Harry Williams has expressed it:

> I believe that many Christians (most notably clergymen) are intellectually dishonest in their attitude to the alleged historical events of the gospel story. As scholars they concede that the historical evidence for this and the other event is doubtful, perhaps sometimes showing beyond reasonable doubt that it never happened. But in church they go on speaking and behaving as though it certainly did and there was absolutely no doubt about it.[22]

While agreeing with Williams's contention that such 'double-think' on the part of the clergy is dishonest and ultimately damaging to the institutional church they serve, there is the problem of the difficulties that clergy face who are honest about their doubts. In the Roman Catholic church, numerous theologians have been deprived for various periods of time of their right to teach, including Hans Küng (Germany), Matthew Fox (USA) and Leonardo Boff (Brazil). And in the Anglican church the clergy who spoke of their doubts on *Heart of the Matter* were summoned by their bishop and asked to apologize, as well as being subject to calls to resign by another bishop and petitions of dissociation by fifteen evangelical clergy from their area.[23] Although part of a less obviously authoritarian ecclesiastical system, Nonconformist clergy can equally find their positions threatened by an attempt at honesty, sometimes with the threat coming from their own congregation (as in the case of Dr Catherine Middleton).[24] Even bishops are sometimes brave enough to speak of their own doubts, although they also discover when they do so the strong weight of conservative religious tradition and its vested power interests. This was well attested in this country in *The Times* obituary for Bishop John Robinson. Under the heading 'Controversial radical theologian' it included the following paragraph:

> His little book *Honest to God* (1963) created a stir partly because he had already generated an expectation that a bishop with such progressive views on sex might upset the apple cart in weightier matters of Christian belief and practice. People were surprised to find a bishop admitting that prayer is difficult, and that some religious language inherited from the past can be more a hindrance than a help.[25]

The current ecclesiastical situation in Germany at the time of writing may illuminate something about the current situation in the West which it would be important to recall as we look at the best options the church has to face as we approach the twenty-first century. Much of what has just been rehearsed might suggest to church leaders that the conservative interpretation is the safest bet, and it would seem that most church authorities have indeed assumed that in times which, politically and economically, may have become more conservative, church-goers would prefer the church to reaffirm traditional verities. But there is evidence to suggest that the opposite may be nearer the case.[26]

We have already referred to the opinion polls in Germany that reveal the extent of secularization in a land which certainly historically and also through the tax-system supposes a basic commitment to Christianity, in both its traditional Western forms — Roman Catholic and Evangelical Protestant (an amalgamation of Lutherans and Calvinists having taken place between 1821 and 1827) — and yet over the past fifteen years some 5 million (as many as the population of the Rhineland) have explicitly withdrawn from ecclesiastical allegiance, so that there are now more atheists than those who attend church. Attendance has now reached an all-time low of 10 per cent of the population of the combined Germanys (with an even lower figure in former East Germany) attending church regularly on Sundays.

The situation was characterized already before he died in 1984 by Germany's greatest Catholic theologian of this century, Karl Rahner SJ, who described his homeland as 'a pagan land with a Christian past and perpetual Christian remnants'. By far the majority of Germans live in places in which it is now remarkable if anyone goes to church on a Sunday. Into this changeable ecclesiastical scenario has entered the colourful figure of Father Eugen Drewermann from Paderborn, a prolific critic of the traditional church and author of over 40 books. Following his confrontation at the end of 1991 with Archbishop Johannes Degenhardt, he was forbidden to teach, preach or exercise his priestly office. In a five-day conference in Karlsruhe in May 1992, which included representation by some 1,400 Catholic organizations, Drewermann became the central figure of debate. After much shilly-shallying, Drewermann was allowed to speak for himself, but only under the conditions set by the hierarchy. These were that he could only speak in discussion with the rigid traditionalist Catholic Hanna-Renate Laurien, and the subject of the debate had to be confined to the Creed. It is clear subsequent to this debate that Drewermann has much support in Germany at large, even within the traditional denominations. A poll of German Catholics showed 58 per cent in his favour with only 34 per cent supporting his adversary, the Archbishop. Among German Protestants polled, the support was understandably even greater, with some 77 per cent in favour of Drewermann and 15 per cent supporting the Archbishop. These figures and this continuing dispute within the traditional churches well illustrate the strong support that exists from those who attend churches for those who hold both radical and critical views.[27]

Although in the English-speaking West there has not until now been such an intense focus for the conflict between traditional and radical believers within the churches, the response received when they speak by more radical bishops (such as David Jenkins in Britain and Jack Spong in the States) as compared with their traditionalist counterparts might well betray a similar situation there. The processes of secularization do not seem to be so very different despite the language-difference.

The case of Drewermann suggests that Christian congregations are not as naïve about questions of belief and doubt as is sometimes supposed by critics of radical positions. It is sometimes argued that non-realist clergy are betraying the trust of their congregations, that their role should be to support traditional teachings rather than to reinterpret them, and that if they do not believe in the literal truth of orthodox doctrines they should resign from their positions of leadership within congregations of believers. But this is to misread seriously the position of clergy within churches, who have always exercised other functions as part of their overall leadership. The pastoral function, for example, is one that is entirely independent of the non-realist question. A member of the clergy can hold to the most orthodox beliefs whilst showing little pastoral care or concern for his or her flock. Equally a most caring pastor can be one who believes that all religious truths are located solely in the realm of the human. Pastoral care is arguably the most important criterion of the success of the clergy (although we must be reminded here of the suggestion by the novelist Graham Greene that priests share with writers the common burden of having no calculable criteria of success) and tests of orthodoxy in belief have certainly always been alien to the Anglican mind. Since Richard Hooker and other formulators of the Anglican ethos in Elizabethan times, the breadth of the teaching of the Established church and its inclusion of much from the differing emphases of Catholic and Protestant traditions has been valued as a distinctive mark of the Anglican ethos. And Samuel Taylor Coleridge in the nineteenth century added in his concept of 'the clerisy' the suggestion that the parish priest of the Church of England represented not only the inherited faith but also in some way the national 'spirituality' of England, whatever flavour that might take at different times. Under such an understanding, one might well produce an argument for a greater number of non-realist clergy to represent the state of the nation at the end of our own secularized twentieth century.

There are also other equally appropriate and established models of the clerical role which would support the continuance of non-realists in their roles of Christian leadership. The clerical profession derived from the role of the rabbi in Jewish society who was regarded not so much as the guardian of the traditions of the faith (that was rather the role of the householder, who conducted most religious rites in the home) as the storyteller *par excellence*, the wandering maverick of wit who would draw people's attention to the spiritual realm by drawing parallels with the material world that was their day-to-day concern. The abiding validity of this ancient model for our society is witnessed by the immense popularity of the East End rabbi Lionel Blue, whose ratings on *Thought for the Day* exceed those of any of his rivals. This particular cleric rehearses no tried and tested certainties but rather seeks to place an ideological bomb under most conventional and commonly held religious doctrines and perspectives. In a similar fashion, his female colleague, Rabbi Julia Neuberger, has achieved media fame through her radical questioning of moral norms rather than a support for traditional ethical positions.

This brings me to the further point that the ordination of women into the ranks of the clergy, which has been effected to various degrees over the past 25 years or so in most Protestant churches, although a process still far from completed there and barely started in Catholic and Orthodox traditions, has introduced a substantially new element into the model or role of the cleric in society. It has been a useful exercise in realizing how far the clerical role has been conceived as inherently masculine. It is a realist objection to the ordination of women that there is a necessary masculine structure in the priesthood and consequently it has been a subsidiary victory for a non-realist perspective that the question of gender is increasingly viewed as culturally relative, rather than as part of an unalterable tradition of order based on biology.

Women in spiritual authority within congregations have been perceived often (though not always) to exercise their ministry in different and not so hierarchical a manner as their male counterparts. The lesson here to be learned is again that of the increasing inevitability, as more women are ordained, of a plurality of models of clerical ministry. Just like non-realist clergy, women by their very nature in this role are critics of the tradition and cannot escape from a vocation of remodelling perceived images of what their contribution is to be to the church as the contemporary community of God in today's society.

A theology which sees the whole church as needing to move over to this way of thinking has recently been provided by Bishop Peter Selby in his challenging book *Belonging*.[28] From seven years' experience of episcopacy in the south of London in the 1980s, the bishop argues that the Church of England as an institution has reverted to a closed and inward-looking club based more on the desire for a *status quo* than for the vision it ought to be sharing with society concerning the nature of human communities. In the bishop's view 'belonging' is a more dynamic image of community than a static 'being' which would hold that the role of the church and its clergy is for ever to maintain the deposit of faith.

There can be little doubt that the Church of England is already involved in a process of radical transition. Even if brought on by no other factors than declining membership and financial stringency, the need for a complete rethink of clerical staffing among other contingencies can be denied no longer. The presence of non-realist clergy and groups such as the Sea of Faith Network provide a dynamic element in the contemporary church as it seeks for greater relevance that can only bode good for an institution that claims to seek truth and be concerned for contemporary social patterns.

If the attenders of the traditional denominational churches are pressing for more contemporary understandings of faith, then it might be useful to conclude this book with a brief sketch of what characteristics we would hope to find in any new understandings in this area. Clearly much has already been hinted in the course of the argument, but a few features will be clear, and are worth specifying.

The first and most important is the theme of this book: faith and doubt are not mutually exclusive but are different aspects of the same dynamic process we know as human believing. Having faith, in others as in ourselves, is for ever an uncertain process and one that causes us unease. We are never quite certain where we stand with other people. All our relationships, even those with our closest family, change as we grow and develop. We grow daily closer to some and further away from others, in ways that are infinitesimally subtle and that involve our subconscious much more than our conscious selves. In the course of individual lives the people we rely on can change many times, in character or in individual *personae*, as our psychological and social needs vary with our circumstances and our situation. Relationships are also by their very nature reciprocal. No matter how much I may want from a particular relationship, it is not achievable unless a similar degree of commitment to it is available by the other person. In a rapidly changing world, I scarcely know my own needs or identity. Small wonder then that I find it difficult to discern those of others. The contemporary relational crisis in the West, revealed starkly in divorce and other family statistics, is humorously illustrated in the films of Woody Allen. Their popularity is due to the fact that in the autobiography of Allen's psychological difficulties and philosophical probings, they touch poignantly on a raw Western nerve. At the end of his film *Annie Hall*, the two main characters meet up again in a café, some time after their sexual relationship had finished. The last words are Alvy's voice-over, as he watches Annie walk away:

> After that it got pretty late. And we both hadda go, but it was great seeing Annie again, right? I realized what a terrific person she was—and how much fun it was just knowing her and I—I thought of that old joke, you know, this—this—this guy goes to a psychiatrist and says, 'Doc, uh, my brother's crazy. He thinks he's a chicken.' And, uh, the doctor says, 'Well, why don't you turn him in?' And the guy says, 'I would, but I need the eggs.' Well, I guess that's pretty much how I feel about relationships. You know, they're totally irrational and crazy and absurd and . . . but, uh, I guess we keep goin' through because, uh, most of us need the eggs.[29]

Non-realism has to be honest in facing the absurdity of many human relationships. We have grown up a lot and come a long way from the comfortable faith of the psalmist when he wrote 'When my father and my mother forsake me, then the Lord will take me up'.[30]

No divine comforter is at hand to give us reassurance. Often in failing and broken relationships, we have to look today to our own spiritual recesses to find the resources to ensure our emotional survival. Believing in ourselves and one another, we have to face up to the reality of much fragmentation and disappointment in our relational lives, while keeping faithful to those who support us and need our presence for them. No longer can the so-called Western nuclear family be set up as the pattern and ideal for all human living. Besides being a statistical minority now in many contemporary urban settings, this idealization betrays far too naïve a conception of the complexity of the human emotional and social life as the findings of modern psychology have now revealed to us. A faith that is open to this truth will want to support and guide those whose close relationships have broken down and who are seeking another configuration for their lives. Relationships must be dynamic and growing if they are to energize, and there needs to be an understanding of them sufficiently intelligent and adaptable to a greater pace of change and a smaller global environment than humankind has ever before been privileged to experience in a single generation.

Another aspect of the 'global village' which all races are now aware of inhabiting together is the understanding we have now achieved of and with other religious traditions. The familiar world of Judaeo-Christianity was historically the religion of only one small sector of the globe, although it always glimpsed the potential for a universal message of human salvation. It never was able to throw off entirely its tribal identity and so perpetuated an incessant and pointless debate about which particular tribal group was the 'true inheritor' of the faith of Abraham. Non-realists have no hesitation in admitting that they all inherited . . . each in their own way. No intellectual striving for supremacy has ultimate validity in a world of multiple value and meaning. Never again can real credence be given to the line of Rudyard Kipling:

> East is East and West is West, and never the twain shall meet.[31]

More hopefully and fruitfully than this, we can become part of the process of 'passing over'[32] from one understanding to another in whatever tradition we find ourselves, and begin to speak with Bede Griffiths (a Benedictine monk who founded an ashram in South India as a prayer centre for people of varying traditions) of 'The Marriage of East and West'. Throughout his life, Griffiths remained committed to a church but only one that can be characterized as an 'open church':

> The building of the church as the manifestation in history of the presence of God in man, is therefore the work of all mankind. The Hindu, the Buddhist, the Muslim, the humanist, the philosopher, the scientist, have all something to give and something to receive. The Christian, to whatever church he may belong, cannot claim to have the monopoly of the Truth.[33]

Christians have to adapt their traditional understandings if they are to take on board just how revolutionary such a new relationship with other traditions really is, just what it implies about truth-claims and our own provisional (rather than ultimate) commitment to our own faith traditions. In an interview she gave following the award of the Booker Prize for Literature for her novel *The Sea, The Sea*,[34] Iris Murdoch welcomed the attempts to merge understandings of religious truth. She revealed of herself:

> I am not a believer in the sense of believing in God the

Father or Jesus Christ as divine. But I believe that religion is terribly important in people's lives, because it tries to look at the world not veiled by the obsessions, fears, and egoism of everyday life. Various priests now tell me that this is what they believe. If only they work fast enough, Christianity can become like Buddhism, before people forget it entirely.[35]

Christians have to take their own initiatives here individually or severally, as to how they are themselves to participate in this new coming together of the traditions and celebrate the new understandings gained. Religious leaders have a responsibility, as in the coming together of the leaders of the traditions at Assisi in 1989, or the decision of the Archbishop of Canterbury in 1992 to withdraw his official patronage of The Church's Mission to the Jews in the light of a developing understanding of dialogue rather than conversion as the operative model of approach. But ordinary church members at the local level can also play their part in cementing newly discovered friendships with the people of other traditions. So in Loughborough, annually in One World Week, all the major Christian denominations participate in a 'Pilgrimage of Prayer for Justice and Peace', at which typically men and women of the traditions living in Loughborough meet together and visit each other's worship-centres in the course of a single evening. From mosque to Sikh temple, Hindu shrine to Raj Yoga household, mediaeval parish church to community centre to meeting with those of Baha'i faith, we can pass through the ecumenical university chapel and conclude in the local Baptist church where in 1991, during the course of the Gulf War, a Muslim led the ceremony of individuals lighting candles with prayer for peace. At each centre, we are welcomed by the leaders of the congregation and we join in the worship of that tradition. Clearly on many occasions we can only participate by observation (if only because of the language difficulty) but that is still what Wittgenstein would call 'a form of religious life' which we can yet venerate even though the dogmas and liturgies remain fairly mysterious to us. The mystery is perhaps not so much in the ceremonies as in the meeting together that such events enable. As we listen, share (worship and often food) and, later, question our host-tradition, we learn together a vital experience of humility often desperately lacking in the monochrome Christian gatherings where everyone appears to believe (and even look) the same. As we take off our shoes or cover our heads in respect of others' customs, we are reminded that we have not come to this worship-centre armed with a superior truth, be it spoken or written. We have come primarily to listen and observe, and so learn more about the complex dynamics of human worship and quest for meaning.

Kenneth Cracknell speaks more tentatively not of 'marriage' but of 'a new relationship', not of 'other faiths' but of 'people of other faith'. Formerly a university Methodist chaplain at Loughborough and later a professional Christian interfaith diplomat travelling 50,000 miles a year on behalf of the British Council of Churches (now the Council of Churches for Britain and Ireland), he has written of the 'provisionality' of all our encounters with other traditions and reminded us that, in contrast to the outmoded former missionary ideals of a superior truth:

> We may not have either a theology or a spirituality which
> is armour plated, an impregnable fortress. The pilgrim
> does not move towards the new age in the spiritual
> equivalent of a Chieftain tank, nor does he or she have
> the spiritual equivalent of a mobile Sainsbury's as logistical
> back-up. Jesus did not say, 'Blessed are those who are
> rich in spirit', any more than he said, 'Those who seek to
> save their souls will save them'.[36]

Inevitably such risky undertakings as pilgrimages across

the world of traditions excite varying emotions. In the Church of England, there was in 1991 something of a backlash to such bold new movements when the Queen attended an interfaith celebration to mark Commonwealth Day at Westminster Abbey. She holds the title 'Defender of the Faith' and opponents of a conciliatory understanding of faith will not tire of reminding us, in their petitions and newspaper columns, of the definite article and of the necessity to defend (at any cost) the deposit of our inherited tribal beliefs which they consider to be the only viewpoint worthy of the description 'Christian'. Jack Spong calls them 'the voices of a dying world-consciousness' and asks of those who would like to see religious truth as somehow located in the monarchy and Westminster Abbey: 'If religious truth cannot exist apart from its national origins, and there is, as yet, no evidence that it can, what will happen when those national origins disappear as they are inevitably bound to do?'[37]

With a shrinking world provided by easier travel, the possibility of meeting across national boundaries has become more realistic, not just for religious leaders but for pilgrims in general. India has become even more consciously the meeting point for the great traditions. Within Christianity itself pilgrimage centres for young people have shot up around monastic centres, such as Taizé in central France and Iona in Scotland. These are places where the rival Western traditions, Catholic and Protestant, can meet together and dispel some of their misconceptions about each other's beliefs. Many of which, of course, derive from an unnecessary continued reliance on realistic frameworks of doctrine.

The acceptance of wider patterns of faith which need not be constructed as mutually contradictory will lead, of course, to freer and more flexible congregations. There will be more stress on experience and less on the worn formulae of the past. Stories of some imaginative content, such as that recounted at the start of this chapter, will be used more than the stale lists of dogmatic precepts recited in the creeds.

Above all, new expressions of faith will give the individual more freedom than in the past. Freedom to choose the expressions of faith and freedom to create the meanings by which individuals choose to live out their personal lives.

Although the metaphor did not please John Selwyn Gummer, Stephen Mitchell on the *Sunday* programme compared the history of faith to the history of art or music, and suggested that to discover our own authentic style of faith we should 'join the painting class'.[38] Such a metaphor suggests that we need a commitment to explore our faith if we are to discover its workings, and as with the other histories it can be a deep and searching process of learning which can lead us to new and challenging ideas. It is important not to shrink from such challenges on the grounds that beliefs are a bedrock, or undergird our lives by their firm truth. Our beliefs are only myths, stories that attempt to illuminate our situation. And by listening to many stories and having our critical judgement of them exercised, we can come to tell our own, and so communicate faith to others. If this sounds a rather solitary and intellectual exercise, it does have such a component, but the story itself does not depend on reason for its impact. The 'painting class' presupposes not only tutors but also fellow pupils, and much of the process of discovery and charting of the waters of the Sea of Faith is most effectively performed together with others. Not *any* others, but those who are prepared to show honesty and courage in sharing both faith and doubt in a very personal and searching way. My experience in the Sea of Faith Network has been that increasing numbers of folk in Britain, as doubtless elsewhere, are wanting to do this, and find the regular area meetings a more satisfactory arena in which to do this than any of the traditional churches.

Possibly one of the problems for churches in Britain, as opposed especially to my experience in the States, is that in concentrating on worship as the ordinary agenda for the gathered community, they have largely ignored the equally important felt need of Christians to educate themselves about and in faith. The only time therefore that the laity meets in a forum in which they can test their theological and ethical ideas is when they are called together in a synod or board which is usually required to vote to effect a policy decision on behalf of the church they are representing. This is scarcely therefore the most appropriate forum for open and honest sharing and exploration, and it is not surprising that many of these meetings become acrimonious in the debate and indecisive in the vote.

As far as the individual is concerned, there is a restlessness in the biblical portrait of the faith of Abraham that is reflected in the contemporary experience of the pilgrimage for meaning. The experience of 'passing over' into other patterns of faith, as described earlier in this chapter, is a dynamic and searching experience, but is not one conducive to allaying such restlessness. Just as the poet Auden after a period making his home sometimes in the Old World, sometimes in the New, began to think of himself as a 'transatlantic Goethe', truly at home in neither continent, so many today have the experience of leaving their home churches in search of another community of faith, but unable to call either their 'home'.

It is not surprising that in the contemporary world with its materialist and consumerist philosophies, those who would search for a deeper meaning to their lives often find themselves lonely and misunderstood. Many are genuinely torn between their quest for spiritual value and the need to compete in the market-place and their materialist ambitions for themselves and their families. At this point it must be remembered that the fee for joining this 'painting class' is somewhat higher than that charged by most local authorities! Indeed, for many it is a price too high for them even to consider.

John S. Dunne quotes a black Spanish saying: 'Those as hunts treasure must go alone, at night, and when they find it they have to leave a little of their blood behind them.'[39] The blood-letting is a process that others have undergone. We can watch how it happened to them, but we cannot escape our own process of wounding. Simone Weil hinted that the reason Kierkegaard might not have achieved his aim was that he remained convinced of the reality of the religious object:

> To go down to the source of our desires, Kierkegaard vainly tried to do so. To go down to the source of our desires in order to tear the energy away from its object. It is there that desires are true, insofar as they are energy. It is the object which is false. But there is an indescribable wrenching apart of the soul at the separation of a desire from its object. The wrenching apart is the condition of truth.[40]

Simone Weil realized in her own life the searing truth she here glimpsed. Like Kierkegaard himself she drifted from one occupation to another, and like him died early (at the age of 34) without having found a spiritual home she could call her own. Yet Weil differs from her nineteenth-century counterpart in one respect that places her clearly in the context of her own century: her spirituality demanded a political aspect, and she gave up the comfort of her family and home to identify with those in great need in her society.

This is a quality Weil shares with many others in the twentieth century. One of its greatest exemplifiers was the Swedish politician who became the first Secretary-General of the United Nations, Dag Hammarskjöld (1905–61), who was born just six months before Dietrich Bonhoeffer and was shot down tragically while on a peace mission to the Congo in 1961. Just before he was killed, on his 53rd birthday, he said to the Jewish philosopher Martin Buber in discussion in New York 'I who stand in the loneliness of a spiritual tower . . . in my great loneliness serve others'. And earlier he had written in his journals, later published as *Markings*: 'In our era the road to holiness necessarily passes through the world of action . . . the longest journey is the journey inwards.'[41] These are the words of a man who professionally had to mediate in some taxing international disputes and who met his death on a journey attempting such a conciliation. And yet he witnessed to the greater challenge that was the inward path, linked to the other, yet unavoidably separate and distinct from it.

I have cited an individual woman and man of our century who each, in their lives and reflections, give us living examples of the kind of vision and faith of a non-realist perspective. Neither of them lived to work out the full implications of their views. Each reveals the truth of our contention in this book. There are no easy answers to questions of faith and doubt. As Paul Tillich best expressed it:

> Faith comprises both itself and the doubt of itself. The
> Christ is Jesus and the negation of Jesus. . . . To live
> serenely and courageously in these tensions and to discover
> finally their ultimate unity in the depths of our own souls
> and in the depth of the divine life is the task and the
> dignity of human thought.[42]

God and spiritual truths are discovered nowhere outside the living and dying of our individual lives. By wrestling with our problems we discover something of our spiritual depth as human beings united by our language and our common search for a fulfilling meaning.

A lot of our expressions, even here, remain deeply rooted in an objective world of Realism which is an outmoded way of seeing things. But we are linguistic creatures and though we play our various language-games we can at least now realize that they *are* games and not reality. We can be conscious that a provisional truth can be adopted and made our own but it has no real meaning beyond that which we assign it. In the course of our lives we shall lock and unlock ourselves into a variety of meaning-systems. But the movement is the substance of our spiritual lives.

The father of the epileptic child spoke for each of us when he said
to Jesus 'I believe; help my unbelief!'[43] Help, not hinder.

Notes

1 David Lodge, *Paradise News* (Secker & Warburg, 1991), p. 280.

2 W. H. Auden, *Secondary Worlds* (Faber, 1968), p. 136.

3 Published as Richard Swinburne, *Faith and Reason* (Clarendon Press, 1981).

4 D. Z. Phillips, 'Wisdom's Gods', *Philosophical Quarterly*, vol. 19 (January 1969).

5 Matthew 13.31f.

6 Anthony Flew, quoted in Peter Donovan, *Religious Language* (Sheldon Press, 1976), p. 18.

7 Rudolf Bultmann, *Faith and Understanding* (SCM, 1969), vol. 1, p. 30.

8 Ibid., p. 132 (a 1927 essay 'On the question of Christology').

9 Adolf Harnack, *Lehrbuch der Dogmengeschichte*, 6th edition (1922), p. 155, quoted by Eric Fromm in *The Dogma of Christ* (Routledge, 1963).

10 Matthew Arnold, 'Dover Beach', quoted in the epigraph of Don Cupitt, *The Sea of Faith: Christianity in Change* (BBC, 1984).

11 Søren Kierkegaard, *Philosophical Fragments* (Princeton University Press, 1967), p. 104.

12 Cf. especially A. J. Ayer, *Language, Truth and Logic* (Penguin, 1971).

13 Ludwig Wittgenstein, *Remarks on Colour* (University of California Press, 1977), para. 317.

14 Mark C. Taylor, *Erring: A Postmodern A/Theology* (University of Chicago Press, 1984), p. 159.

15 Roland Barthes, *Empire of Signs* (Hill & Wang, 1982), p. 78.

16 John 20.28. The ecclesiastical use of this image is exemplified in the then Archbishop of Canterbury's official response to Bishop John Robinson's *Honest to God*. See Michael Ramsey, *Image Old and New* (SPCK, 1963), p. 14.

17 Richard L. Rubenstein, *After Auschwitz: History, Theology and Contemporary Judaism* (Johns Hopkins University Press, 1992).

18 Erik Erikson, *Insight and Responsibility* (Faber, 1966), p. 85.

19 In his autobiographical *Words* (Penguin, 1964), quoted in Peter Hebblethwaite's article about Sartre and religion in *The Times* (1 October 1977) under the provocative title 'The great yawn of a soul chosen for doubt and despair'.

20 Miguel de Unamuno, *Perplexities and Paradoxes* (Philosophical Library, 1945), pp. 2f.

21 Don Cupitt, 'Fundamentalism and the 200-year credibility gap', *The Guardian* (22 August 1992).

22 Harry Williams, *Some Day I'll Find You* (Mitchell Beazley, 1982), p. 370.

23 Ruth Gledhill, 'Bishop tells doubting clergy to resign', *The Times* (20 April 1992). Cf. also 'Holy row is resurrected', *Loughborough Mail* (14 May 1992).

24 Ibid.

25 *The Times* (7 November 1983). Cf. similar controversy amongst American bishops following Bishop Spong's ordination to the priesthood of an open lesbian and his defence of this and other 'progressive views' on sex, in *Living in Sin?* (Harper, 1990).

26 In addition, Don Cupitt has questioned whether, in the present Western pluralist culture, fundamentalism in the old sense can even be deemed to exist, other than as a description of people who select particular biblical texts for their particular purposes. He argues: 'The old skill of living by the book can no longer exist as it did until the nineteenth century, because the culture has changed'; cf. *Radicals and the Future of the Church* (SCM, 1984), p. 170.

27 Cf. *Der Spiegel* (25/1992), pp. 36–57.

28 Peter Selby, *Belonging: Challenge to a Tribal Church* (SPCK, 1991).

29 In *Four Films of Woody Allen* (Faber, 1983), p. 105.

30 Psalm 27.10 (Authorized Version).

31 As quoted (and subsequently demolished) in the introduction to Harvey Cox, *Turning East* (Simon & Schuster, 1977), p. 7.

32 John S. Dunne, *The Way of All the Earth: An Encounter with Eastern Religions* (Sheldon Press, 1973).

33 Bede Griffiths, *The Marriage of East and West* (Collins, 1982), pp. 202f.

34 Iris Murdoch, *The Sea, The Sea* (Chatto & Windus, 1978).

35 *The Times* (23 November 1978).

36 Kenneth Cracknell, *Towards a New Relationship: Christians and People of Other Faith* (Epworth, 1986), p. 149.

37 Bishop John Shelby Spong, *The Future of Christianity in the West* (Loughborough University, 1992), p. 16.

38 On BBC Radio 4 on Easter Day 1992. Cf. Charles Moore, 'Mr Gummer and the jellyfish on Dover Beach', *The Spectator* (25 April 1992).

39 Quoted in John S. Dunne, *The Reasons of the Heart* (Macmillan, 1978), p. 55.

40 Simone Weil, *Gravity and Grace* (Routledge, 1963), p. 20.

41 Dag Hammarskjöld, *Markings* (Faber, 1964), pp. 108, 65.

42 Paul Tillich, *Biblical Religion and the Search for Ultimate Reality* (University of Chicago Press, 1955), p. 85.

43 Mark 9.24.

Index of Names

Index of Subjects